Helen's
Copy & Use
Quilting Patterns

HELEN SQUIRE

For Betty —
may you quilt
in peace.
Helen Squire
Paducah, KY 2009

American Quilter's Society
P. O. Box 3290 • Paducah, KY 42002-3290
www.AQSquilt.com

Dear Helen Series • Book Six

Located in Paducah, Kentucky, the American Quilter's Society (AQS) is dedicated to promoting the accomplishments of today's quilters. Through its publications and events, AQS strives to honor today's quiltmakers and their work and to inspire future creativity and innovation in quiltmaking.

EDITOR: HELEN SQUIRE

GRAPHIC DESIGN & ILLUSTRATIONS: LYNDA SMITH

COVER DESIGN & ILLUSTRATIONS: MICHAEL BUCKINGHAM

PHOTOGRAPHY: CHARLES R. LYNCH

Library of Congress Cataloging-in-Publication Data
Helen Squire
      Helen's Copy and Use Quilting Designs / by Helen Squire
        p. cm.
     ISBN 1-57432-790-9
   1. Quilting--Patterns I. Title: Helen's copy and use quilting
patterns. II. Title: Copy & use quilting patterns. III. Title.
   TT835 .S6667 2002
     746.46'041--dc21

                  2001008440

Additional copies of this book may be ordered from the American Quilter's Society, PO Box 3290, Paducah, KY 42002-3290, or online at www.AQSquilt.com.

Dedication

To Robby Wargny of New Port Richie, Florida, and students like her, who take classes and then far surpass the teacher's ideas.

To Theresa Fleming of Aurora, Colorado, a student who introduced me almost a decade ago to the need for flowing designs for machine quilters.

To Michael Buckingham and Lynda Smith, my co-workers at AQS, whose artistic and graphic-design talents make my quilting patterns sing!

To Laura Kearns Stamm, Susan Squire, and Vanessa Kaiser, my wonderful daughters, who grew up thinking all mothers work at a lightbox with a cup of tea nearby.

To my sisters, Rickey, Flo, Trudy, Jeanne, and Barbara, and my best friends, Marian Piehler and Joyce Lockatell, who gave me unconditional encouragement.

Contents

Introduction **6**

Quilting Decisions **7**

How to Use the Patterns **8**

Chapter One   **Helen's Hints** **9**

Cupid's Heart, Cupid's Curl, Helene, Greek Key, Wedding Ring Hearts, Nancy, Quilted Star, Flo's Feathered Plumes, Mardi Gras Celebration

Chapter Two   **Circular Styles** **18**

Georgina, Feathered Wreath with Grid, Feathers & Circles Wreath, Peony Wreath, Elegant Swirl, Captain Syd's Porthole, Double Feathers, New Orleans Wreath, New Orleans Machine, Wheel of Lilies, Americana, Grecian Sun, Fanfare

Chapter Three   **Sweetheart Designs** **36**

Megan, Caroline, Judi's Left-Handed Tulip Wreath, Lindajean's Garden, Julie's Tulip Border, Tulip Patch Border, Tulip Patch Block, Lillian's Candy Box Bows, Jinny Variation, Climbing Clematis, Peaceful Birds, Trudy's Bows, Dolly's Paper Cut-outs, Jeanine's Miniature, Jeanine's Rope Heart, Philodendron Sashing, Lucky Kisses, Heart & Bow, Embossed Heart, Entwined Hearts, Loving Kisses, My Heart Belongs to Baby

Chapter Four   **Sashing Strips** **52**

Twist & Turn Daffodils, Betty's Twist & Turn, Penelope's Plumes, Stella's Delight, Pumpkin Seed, Caroline's Lattice, Elba's Star Flowers, Green's Garden, Frank's Flower, Angela's Ribbon, Elisa's Posies and Grid, Bab's Berries, Aimee's Chain, Double Feather Border, Daphne's Laurel

Contents

Chapter Five   **Borders & Blocks** **64**

Bud's Rope & Cable, Carla's Conch Variations, Lynda's Heart Block, Ocotillo's Border, Fred's Maze, Strawberries on the Vine, Rickey, Ornament Sashing, Poinsettia Block, Holly Bells Block, Winter White, Blue Ice, Holiday Border, Overlapping Circles, Overlapping Ovals, Viola's Vine, Doug's Design, Laura's Cable, Monica

Chapter Six   **Fun Patterns** **88**

Michael's Circus Tent, Teddy Bear, Panda, Lion Cub, Tiger Cub, Seahorse, Dancing Dolphins, Buck's Boat, Whale, Pearl's Shells, School Fish, Charlie, Mermaid, Octopus, Snail, Mushroom Border, Leap Frog, Costa Rica, Argentina, Trinidad, Birds & Flowers, Vanessa's Butterfly, Turtle Back Zoo, Butterfly Collection

Chapter Seven   **Continuous Lines** **106**

Barbara, Jeanne, Florence, Carter's Crown, Little Angel, Cupid's Wings, Lisabeth's Corner, Lisabeth's Variation, Koren's Border, Elizabeth, Lisabeth's Long-arm, Lisabeth's Wreath, Princess Sasa, Donald's Kingdom, Cloud Nine Variations, Sweetheart Corner, Baby Sweetheart, Marilyn, Carolyn, Shelley's Loving Cup

Chapter Eight   **Elegant Sets** **124**

Theresa's Scroll & Leaf, Elegant Block, Elegant Sashings and Corner, Lily Pad, Elegant Corners, Elegant Rope, Elegant Rope, Elegant Heart Center, Francine, Posie Basket, Phyllis, Phil's Wreath, Abbie's Ocean Waves, Manie's Maui, Surfs Up Continuous Line

Chapter Nine   **Grids VI** **138**

Pumpkin Seed, ½" Crosshatch, 1" Crosshatch, ¾" Crosshatch, Gladys' Rose

Introduction

This book, *Helen's Copy & Use Quilting Patterns,* is a direct response both to the needs of today's quilter for more and more patterns, in a variety of sizes, and suitable for traditional-looking quilts, and to the necessity of having extra copies for pre-planning one's quilting layout. Add in the fact that quilters are combining hand quilting with sewing machine quilting and doing sit-down or stand-up machine quilting, and it becomes apparent that a different type of pattern book was mandated.

My designs are protected by copyright and are highly visible in the quilting community, and copies of the patterns themselves may not be resold. However, any person buying the *Dear Helen* quilting book series has my permission to make multiple copies, photocopies and scans of the patterns included, for their personal use. Commercial quilters-for-hire and professional quilters have the right to include my patterns in their repertoire of designs shown to their customers. My patterns appear regularly in national magazine articles, and are available and sold as plastic stencils, pantographs, peel & stick patterns, pre-marked kits, and stamped wholecloth fabric.

If you enter quilt show competitions where the rules stipulate that you identify the fabrics, pattern, and quilting sources, a simple "inspired by Helen Squire's pattern Viola's Vine" (shown here and on the cover) would suffice. As you read this book and follow my advice, you will develop your own ideas about using the patterns, and therefore, the final adaptation is entirely your own creation. You should take the praise, not I.

I was both happy and sad when AQS and I discussed reprinting or discontinuing the large, spiralbound copies of the *Dear Helen* series since they are labor intensive, heavy to ship, and hard to display in stores. Instead, we decided to include some of the most popular patterns in a new, multi-page book format. At first, I was disappointed that the printed-one-side-only, 17" x 11" oversize format, which allowed bigger blocks and longer patterns, would be replaced by a standard 8½" x 11" page. However, I was pleased to have the opportunity to redraft my original patterns into newer sizes with more variations and, yes, to adapt some patterns for machine quilting. For *Dear Helen, Ask Helen,* and *Show Me Helen,* I had hand drawn each quilting dash! Now they can be computer generated and more accurately drawn, as they were in *Helen's Guide* and *Create with Helen.*

I hope you enjoy every stitch.

Helen Squire

Quilting Decisions

Whether you quilt by hand or machine, the same quilting decisions will apply. Pre-planning the quilting areas means considering the fabric, the size of each piece, and how seam allowances are pressed <u>before</u> you start. This quilt is a good example of the variety of areas to be considered...

Appliqué motif
Outline quilting around the shape enhances the design.

Gridlines
Diagonal crosshatch – structural quilting that holds the batting flat.

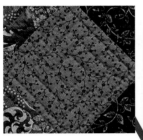

Outer border
Echo, contour quilting within the pieced shape.

Inner border
Quilting follows the precision-cut fabric motif without marking.

Border width
Size of the quilting pattern depends on how seams are pressed underneath.

Patchwork
In-the-ditch quilting along the side without extra seam allowances.

Teapot Bouquet, 56" x 56", by Robby Wargny.
She showcases Nancy Pearson's appliqué pattern #98 (used by permission), and my Viola's Vine quilting pattern, pages 80 and 81.

Corner block
Fancy quilting design is lost in the busy print fabric.

Main border
Showcases stitches – the quilting design is pre-planned to reverse at the center.

How to Use the Patterns

A combined total of 275 patterns, placement diagrams, and reversed designs in a variety of sizes are in this book. Enlargement charts for the most popular sizes are provided (see pages 20 – 21, 47, and 89). More importantly, determining the area to be quilted is discussed.

The quilting patterns have been loosely grouped into the following seven categories: *Circular Styles, Sweetheart Designs, Sashing Strips, Borders & Blocks, Fun Patterns, Continuous Lines,* and *Elegant Sets.* There are more pattern types in *Helen's Hints* and *Grids VI.* The entire book overlaps. Each chapter contains some continuous-line patterns that can be quilted by short or long-arm machines. There are sashing strips that have borders, and borders included for fun! Hearts and tulips are everyone's favorites and appear throughout the book.

Known for folding patterns into perfect miters, I use the same trial-and-error steps for all of my repetitive pattern designs. I have demonstrated my methods on various television shows, including *Simply Quilts, Sew Creative, Quilt Central,* and *QVC Shopping Network.* Now, let me show you how it's done.

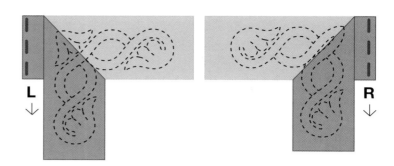

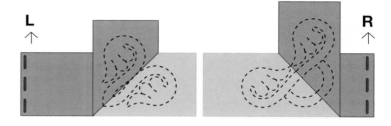

- ☐ Layer two copies facing together. Staple patterns at either end, then fold where you like the design. At least four different versions are always possible.

- ☐ Select the design you want and redraw an accurate copy.

- ☐ Make three or more copies, positioning this new design in borders, sashing, or block areas. Enlarge or reduce to fit the area to be quilted.

- ☐ For pre-planning, there are three places to begin positioning the quilting design: ❶ in the corner, ❷ in the center, or ❸ midway in-between, such as swags.

- ☐ You need three copies of the design and one of them should be the reversed image. They may not all be used, but having them gives you more choices.

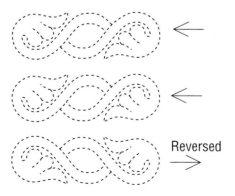

Reversed

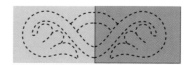

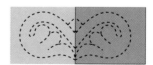

- ☐ Center reversals are easy to fold and can be adapted to fit any border or block measurement.

- ☐ Refer to *Sashing Strips*, page 53, *Borders & Blocks*, page 68, and *Continuous Lines*, page 116-117, for other step-by-step examples of how to use the patterns.

Chapter One

Helen's Hints

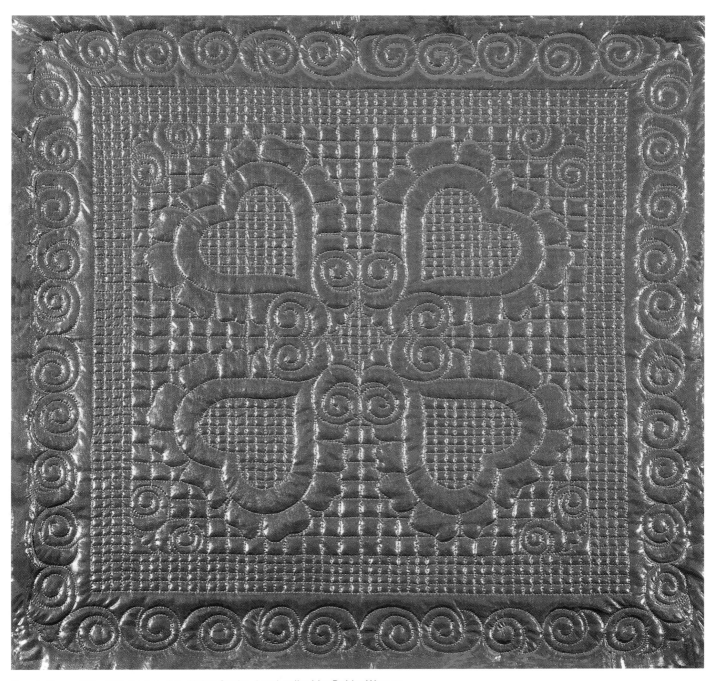

CUPID'S HEART, 31" x 31", designed by Helen Squire, hand quilted by Robby Wargny.

❑ A touch of elegance is added to the *CUPID'S HEART* quilt with imitation gold lamé on the front and a theme fabric in red and gold on the back.

❑ The essence of the pattern is the swirl design called *Cupid's Curl.* Once an element or motif is identified, it can easily become the basis for coordinated border and block designs.

❑ The full patterns for *Cupid's Heart, Cupid's Curl,* and the latest variation, *Heavenly Clouds,* are on pages 10 and 11.

❑ The quilting patterns for *Cloud Nine Continuous, Cloud Nine Appliqué Variation,* and *Cloud Nine Sashing* are found in *Continuous Lines,* pages 118 and 119.

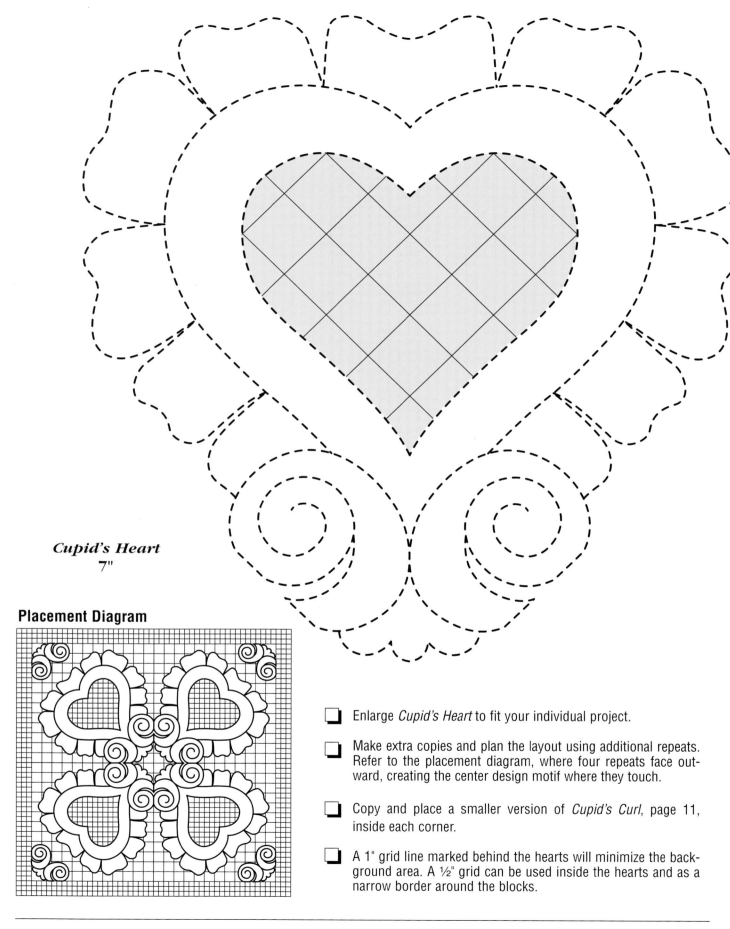

Cupid's Heart
7"

Placement Diagram

☐ Enlarge *Cupid's Heart* to fit your individual project.

☐ Make extra copies and plan the layout using additional repeats. Refer to the placement diagram, where four repeats face outward, creating the center design motif where they touch.

☐ Copy and place a smaller version of *Cupid's Curl*, page 11, inside each corner.

☐ A 1" grid line marked behind the hearts will minimize the background area. A ½" grid can be used inside the hearts and as a narrow border around the blocks.

Placement Diagram: Multiple repeats form a new block, *Heavenly Clouds*. Shaded detail was added to outside corners.

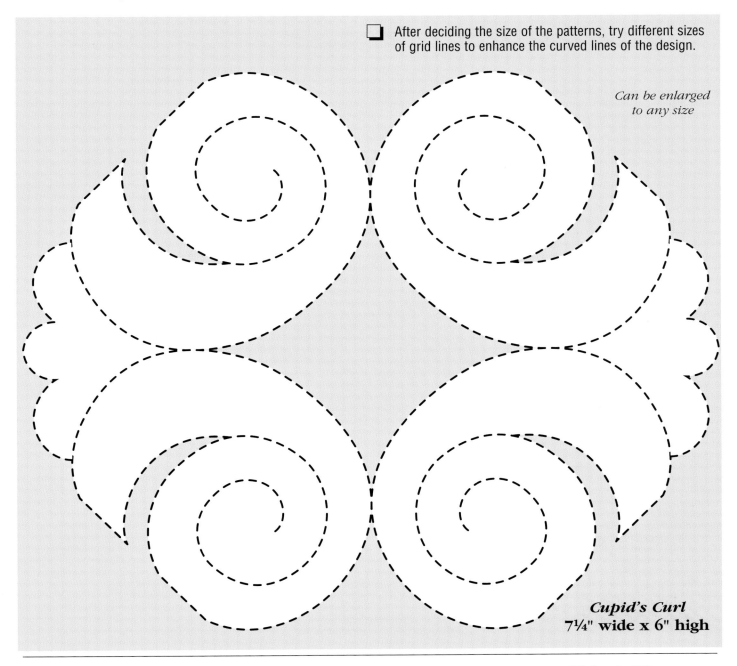

After deciding the size of the patterns, try different sizes of grid lines to enhance the curved lines of the design.

Can be enlarged to any size

Cupid's Curl
7¼" wide x 6" high

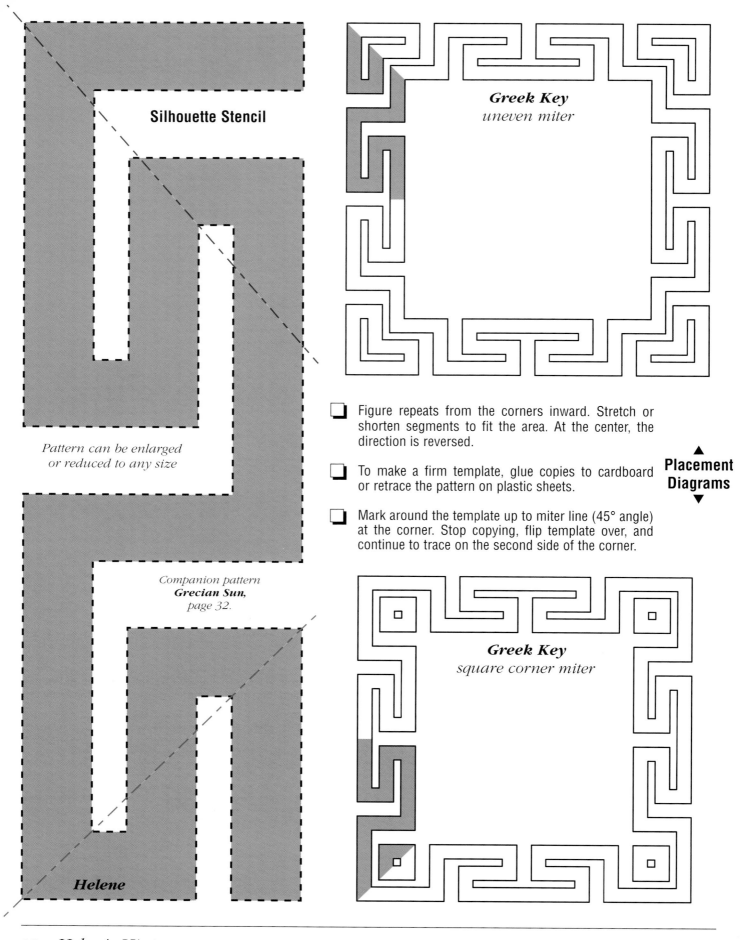

Silhouette Stencil

Pattern can be enlarged or reduced to any size

Companion pattern
Grecian Sun,
page 32.

Helene

Greek Key
uneven miter

Figure repeats from the corners inward. Stretch or shorten segments to fit the area. At the center, the direction is reversed.

To make a firm template, glue copies to cardboard or retrace the pattern on plastic sheets.

Mark around the template up to miter line (45° angle) at the corner. Stop copying, flip template over, and continue to trace on the second side of the corner.

▲
**Placement
Diagrams**
▼

Greek Key
square corner miter

Wedding Ring Hearts
6"

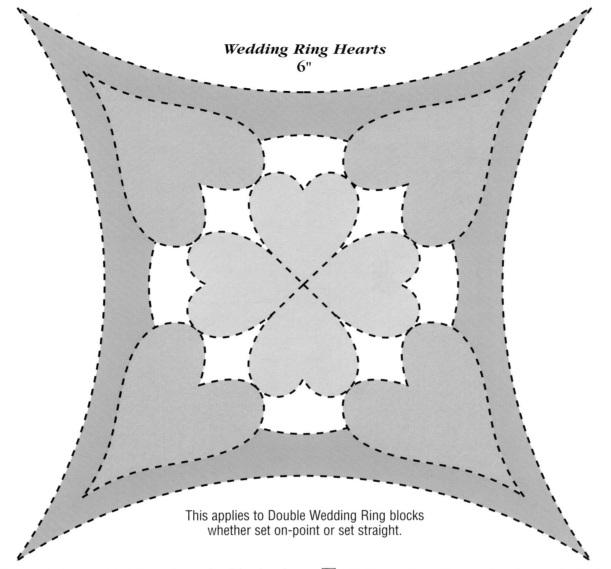

This applies to Double Wedding Ring blocks
whether set on-point or set straight.

1 A flowing design used in intersections of solid-colored pieces show off your quilting stitches nicely.

2 It's easier to quilt in the ditch with the seams pressed to one side, along the pieced "melon" wedges.

3 Quilting in the background fabric very close to the seams will raise up the circular shape of the rings.

4 Outline quilting ¼" around each piece is the traditional choice, but this does little to enhance the overall design.

5 On larger quilt patterns, you can add a fancy shape inside the crescent to coordinate with the center design.

6 Hearts & flowers motifs are lovely choices for all Double Wedding Ring quilts. Enlarge the pattern to fit the opening.

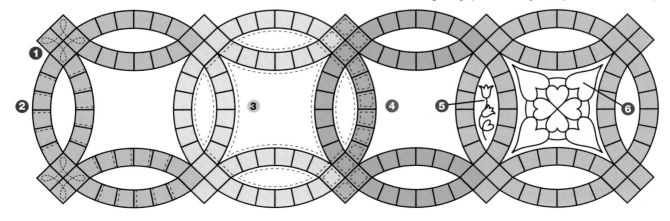

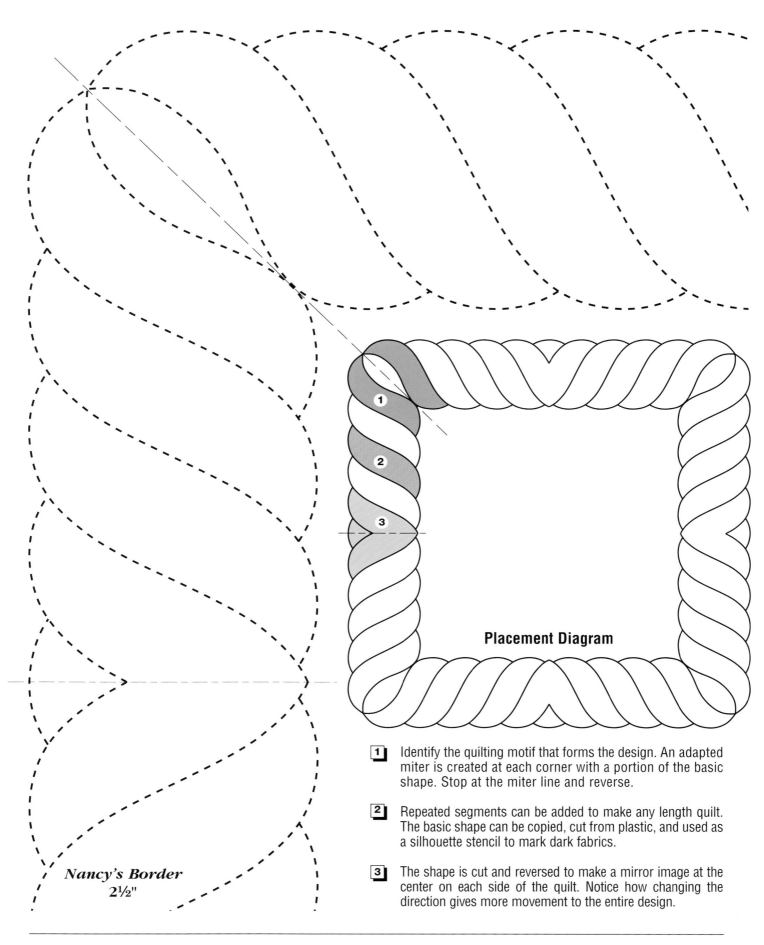

Placement Diagram

Nancy's Border
2½"

1 Identify the quilting motif that forms the design. An adapted miter is created at each corner with a portion of the basic shape. Stop at the miter line and reverse.

2 Repeated segments can be added to make any length quilt. The basic shape can be copied, cut from plastic, and used as a silhouette stencil to mark dark fabrics.

3 The shape is cut and reversed to make a mirror image at the center on each side of the quilt. Notice how changing the direction gives more movement to the entire design.

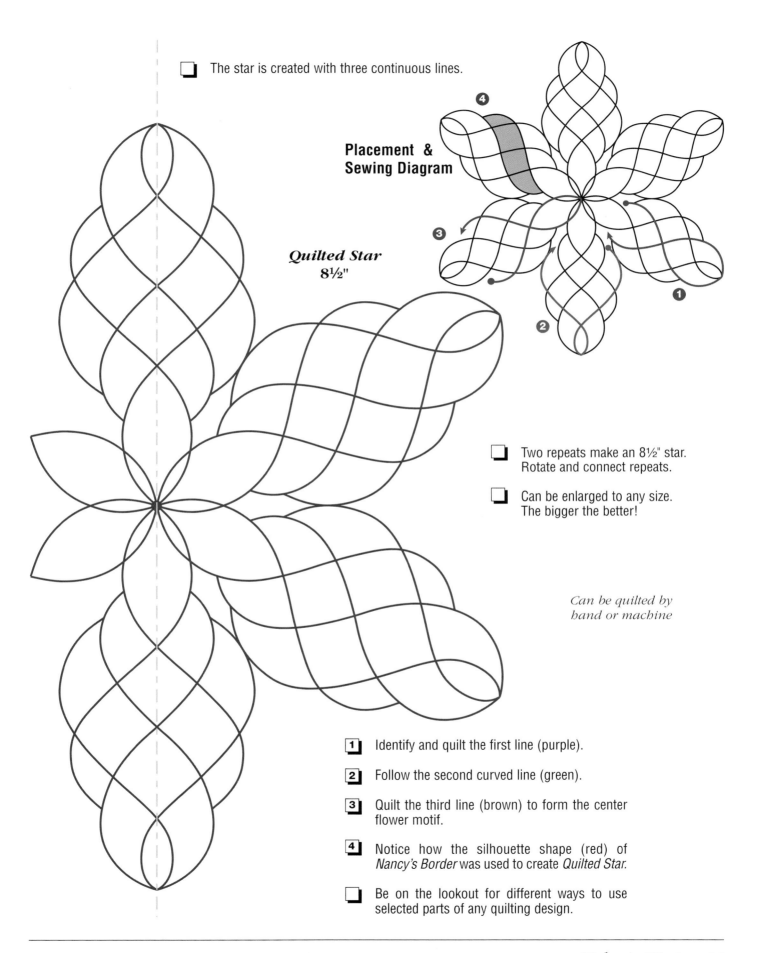

The star is created with three continuous lines.

Placement & Sewing Diagram

Quilted Star
8½"

Two repeats make an 8½" star. Rotate and connect repeats.

Can be enlarged to any size. The bigger the better!

Can be quilted by hand or machine

1 Identify and quilt the first line (purple).

2 Follow the second curved line (green).

3 Quilt the third line (brown) to form the center flower motif.

4 Notice how the silhouette shape (red) of *Nancy's Border* was used to create *Quilted Star*.

Be on the lookout for different ways to use selected parts of any quilting design.

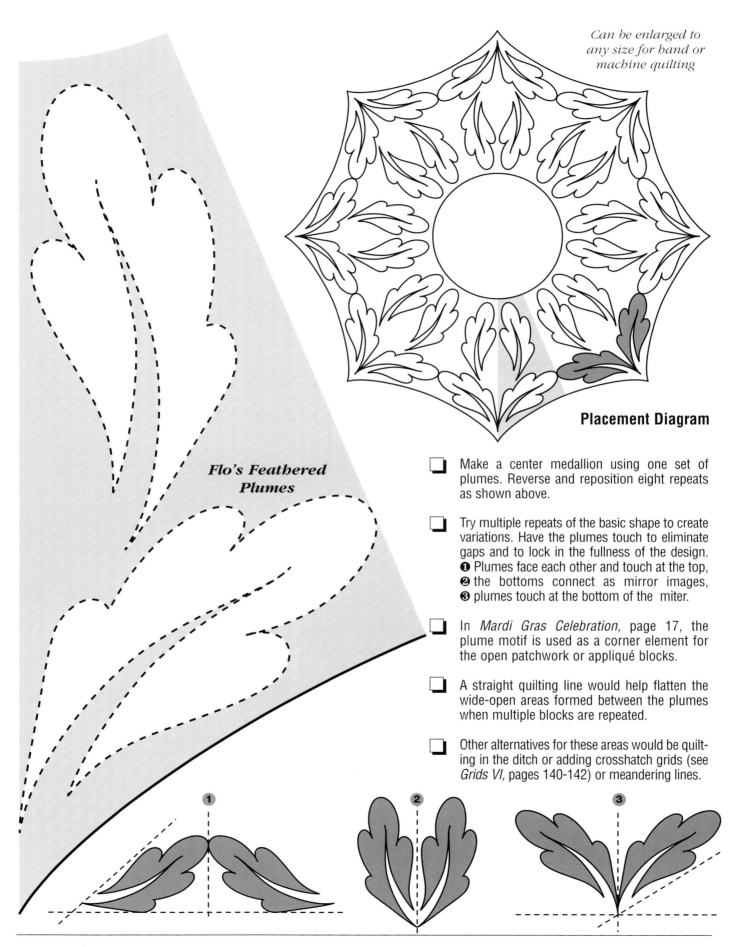

Can be enlarged to any size for hand or machine quilting

Placement Diagram

Flo's Feathered Plumes

☐ Make a center medallion using one set of plumes. Reverse and reposition eight repeats as shown above.

☐ Try multiple repeats of the basic shape to create variations. Have the plumes touch to eliminate gaps and to lock in the fullness of the design.
❶ Plumes face each other and touch at the top, ❷ the bottoms connect as mirror images, ❸ plumes touch at the bottom of the miter.

☐ In *Mardi Gras Celebration,* page 17, the plume motif is used as a corner element for the open patchwork or appliqué blocks.

☐ A straight quilting line would help flatten the wide-open areas formed between the plumes when multiple blocks are repeated.

☐ Other alternatives for these areas would be quilting in the ditch or adding crosshatch grids (see *Grids VI,* pages 140-142) or meandering lines.

Mardi Gras Celebration

▲
Placement Diagrams
▼

Chapter Two

Circular Styles

- Circular designs are the "whipped cream" of quilting. They are easier to quilt because they are typically used in plain blocks without seam allowances.

- This is the perfect place to showcase your finest quilting stitches. Feathered wreaths and circular designs are always noticed. They command attention.

- Did you know that there are right and left directions for every wreath, and that they are quilted clockwise or counter-clockwise?

- Clockwise patterns are easier for right-handed quilters. Counter-clockwise patterns are better for left-handed quilters or machine quilting. Finger trace the one that is best for you.

- In this book, and especially in this chapter, both directions are provided. One may be featured larger, but the alternative is provided to be enlarged as needed.

- The enlargement and reduction charts for popular circular sizes are given on pages 20 and 21.

- Some circular patterns have been included in other chapters. Shown on this page are patterns that make a circle when elements are repeated.

- Size is the most important part of selecting an appropriate pattern. See *Americana*, page 31, for examples of determining the placement or area to be quilted.

Cupid's Wings
As shown in *Continuous Lines*, page 111

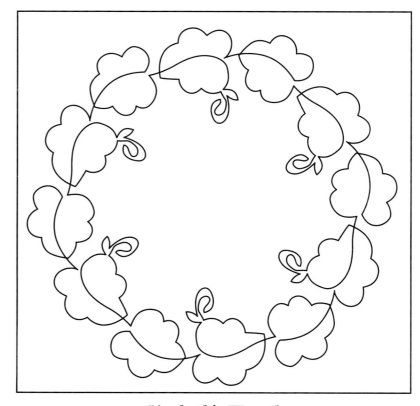

Lisabeth's Wreath
As shown in *Continuous Lines*, page 115

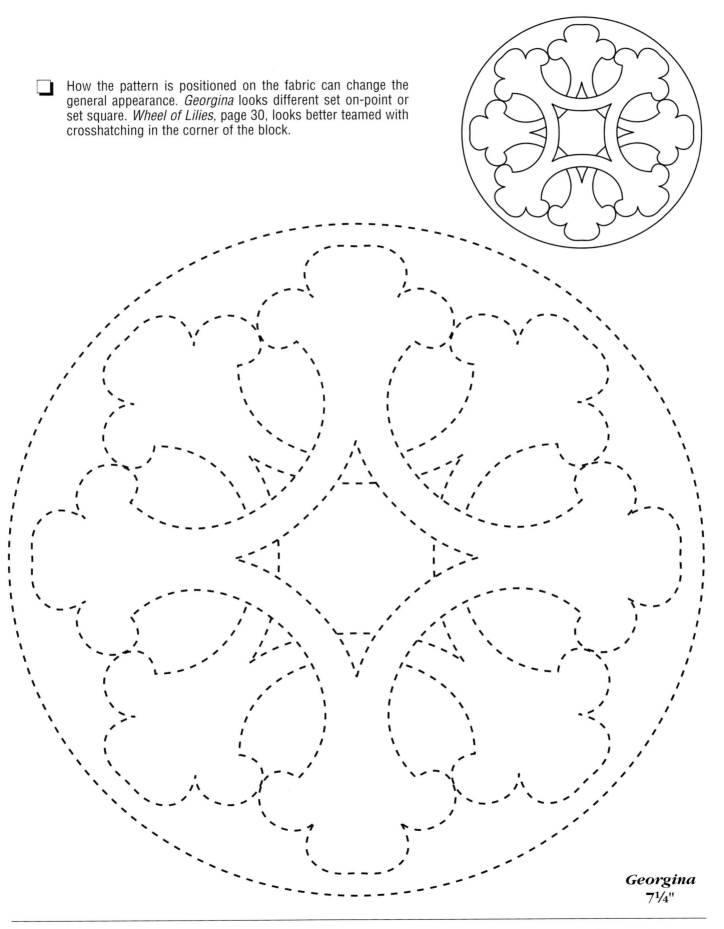

How the pattern is positioned on the fabric can change the general appearance. *Georgina* looks different set on-point or set square. *Wheel of Lilies,* page 30, looks better teamed with crosshatching in the corner of the block.

Georgina
7¼"

Feathered Wreath with Grid, page 22

Feathers & Circles Wreath, page 23

Peony Wreath, page 24

Captain Syd's Porthole, page 26

To enlarge these patterns you can measure the square as shown, or measure the diameter of the circular design on pages 22–33.

Be aware of underlying seams and allow proper space to prevent quilting through those extra thicknesses. For white-work quilts, machine quilting, and individual blocks, this is not necessary.

Measure from side to side or top to bottom to determine the percentage of enlargement needed. For standard size blocks, use the following charts:

3⅝" ENLARGED TO	4"	=	E 110%
3⅝" ENLARGED TO	5"	=	E 142%
3⅝" ENLARGED TO	5½"	=	E 152%
3⅝" ENLARGED TO	6"	=	E 165%

Double Feathers, page 28

New Orleans Wreath, page 29

Grecian Sun, page 32

Fanfare, page 33

For 7" wreaths: 7" ENLARGED TO 7½" = E 107%
7" ENLARGED TO 8" = E 114%
7" ENLARGED TO 8½" = E 121%
7" ENLARGED TO 9" = E 129%
7" ENLARGED TO 10" = E 143%
7" ENLARGED TO 11" = E 157%
7" ENLARGED TO 12" = E 172%

For 7½" wreaths: 7½" REDUCED TO 7" = R 93%
7½" ENLARGED TO 8" = E 106%
7½" ENLARGED TO 8½" = E 113%
7½" ENLARGED TO 9" = E 120%
7½" ENLARGED TO 10" = E 134%
7½" ENLARGED TO 11" = E 147%
7½" ENLARGED TO 12" = E 160%

I recommend purchasing a proportional scale ruler. They take the math out of resizing. Line up the measurement of the design you have on the inner ring and dial what you want on the outside ring. The increase or reduction amount shows in a window opening as a percentage.

Available at quilt shops, wallpaper and art supply stores, or order directly from Golden Threads, 2 S. 373 Seneca Drive, Wheaton, IL 60187. Website: www.goldenthreads.com. Price: $6.00 retail.

Feather Wreath with Grid
7"

Standard photocopiers have pre-set reductions of 77%, 85%, 93%, and pre-set enlargements of 110%, 121%, or 150%. Average the size of adjustments to the closest setting.

Make a copy and reproduce that enlargement or reduction as many times as necessary to obtain the size needed.

Feathers & Circles Wreath
7"

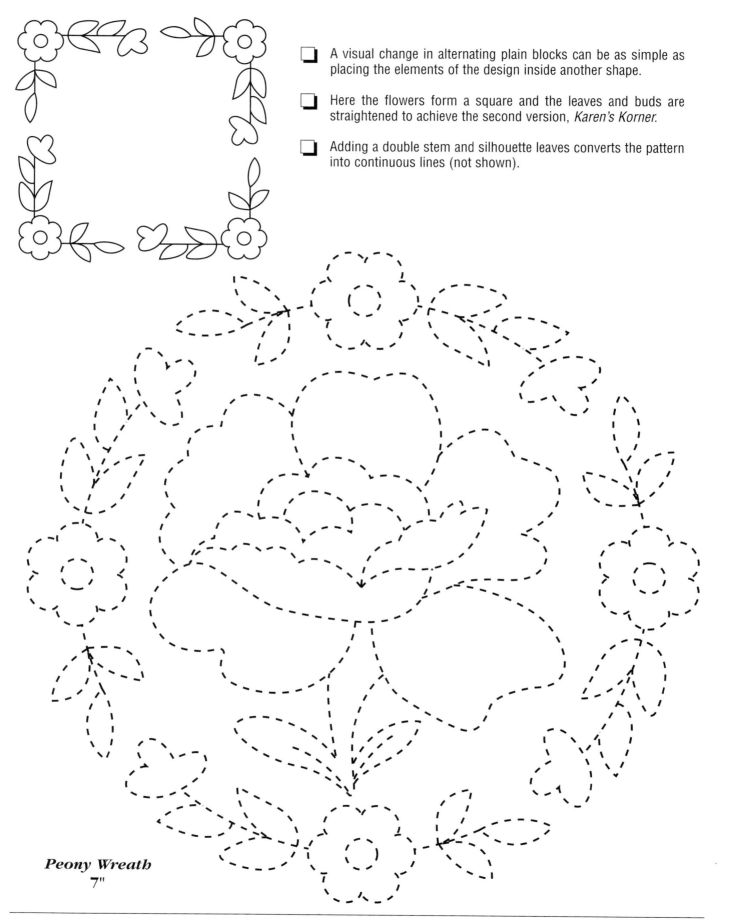

- A visual change in alternating plain blocks can be as simple as placing the elements of the design inside another shape.

- Here the flowers form a square and the leaves and buds are straightened to achieve the second version, *Karen's Korner.*

- Adding a double stem and silhouette leaves converts the pattern into continuous lines (not shown).

Peony Wreath
7"

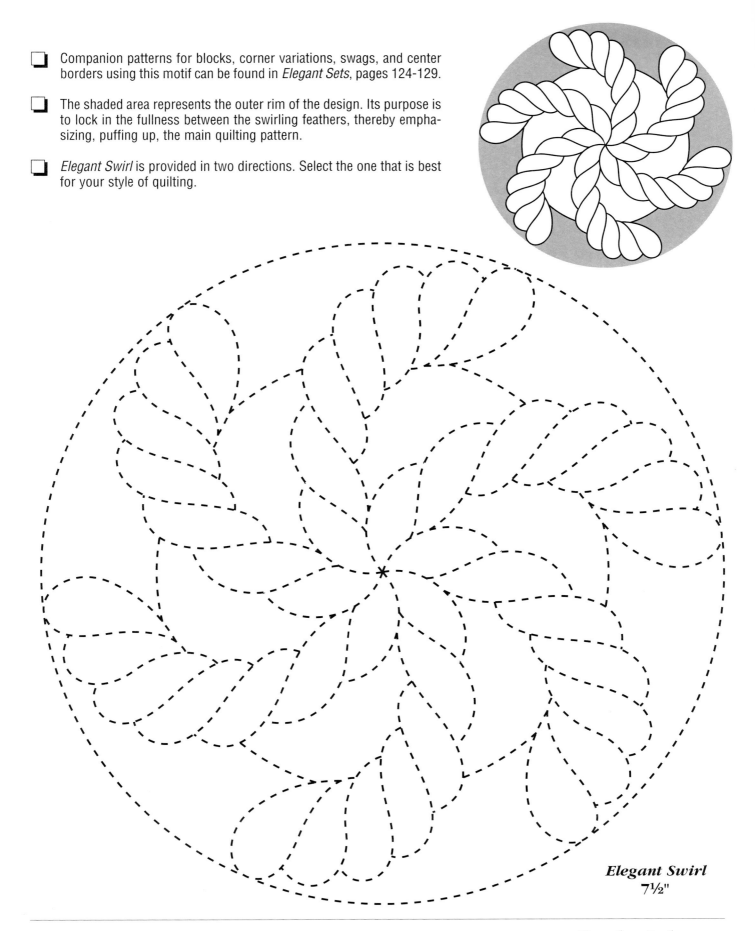

- Companion patterns for blocks, corner variations, swags, and center borders using this motif can be found in *Elegant Sets*, pages 124-129.

- The shaded area represents the outer rim of the design. Its purpose is to lock in the fullness between the swirling feathers, thereby emphasizing, puffing up, the main quilting pattern.

- *Elegant Swirl* is provided in two directions. Select the one that is best for your style of quilting.

Elegant Swirl
7½"

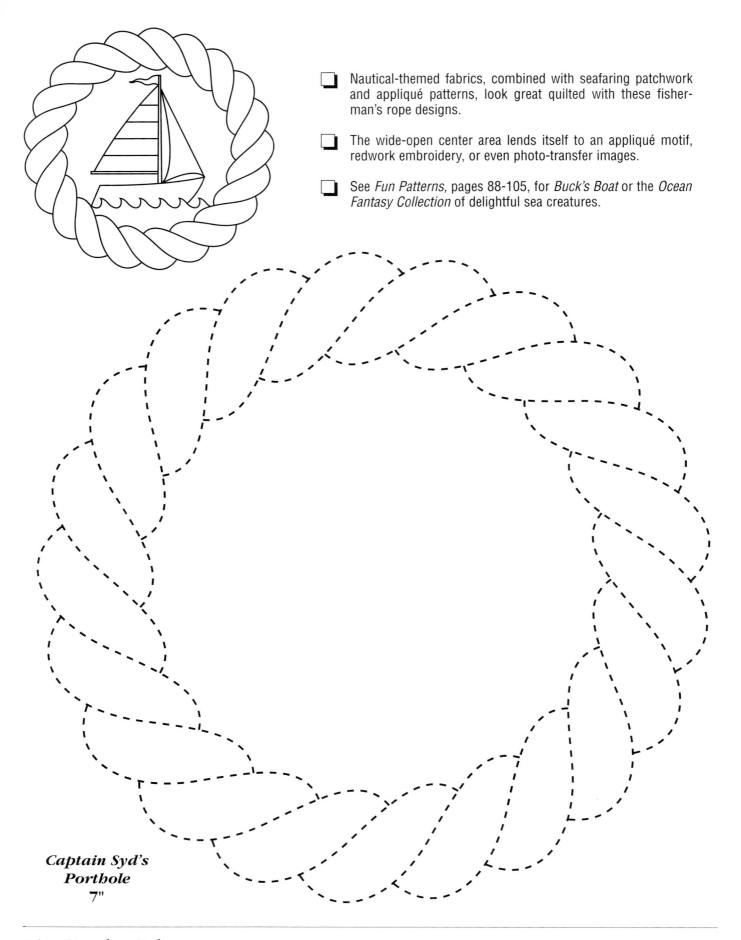

Nautical-themed fabrics, combined with seafaring patchwork and appliqué patterns, look great quilted with these fisherman's rope designs.

The wide-open center area lends itself to an appliqué motif, redwork embroidery, or even photo-transfer images.

See *Fun Patterns,* pages 88-105, for *Buck's Boat* or the *Ocean Fantasy Collection* of delightful sea creatures.

Captain Syd's Porthole
7"

- All of my patterns are named after my family, friends, or places where I derive inspiration.

- The Piehler family especially influenced my heart-shaped *Jeanie's Heart* pattern. It was designed using *Bud's Rope Cable*, page 65. After Bud died, Marian wanted to make a wedding quilt for their daughter, Jeanie. This simple-looking shape took me days to create and is one of my favorite patterns.

- Heart shapes should be measured by the total area they fill – the height and the width. More information on enlarging rectangles is on page 89.

- Shading in the background area helps you visualize the background's effects on the main design.

Companion patterns include
Jeanie's Rope Heart, *page 46 and*
Bud's Rope Cable, *page 65.*

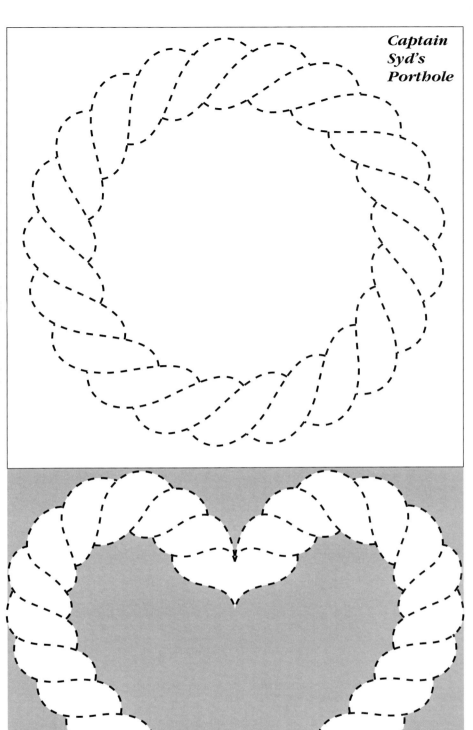

*Captain
Syd's
Porthole*

Jeanie's Heart

Double Feathers 7"

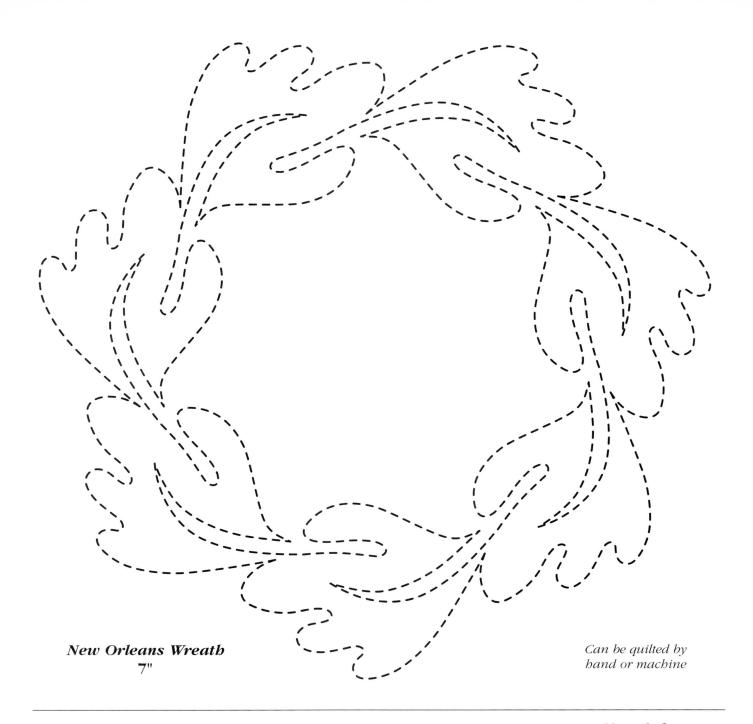

New Orleans Wreath
7"

*Can be quilted by
hand or machine*

**New Orleans
Machine Quilting**
2"

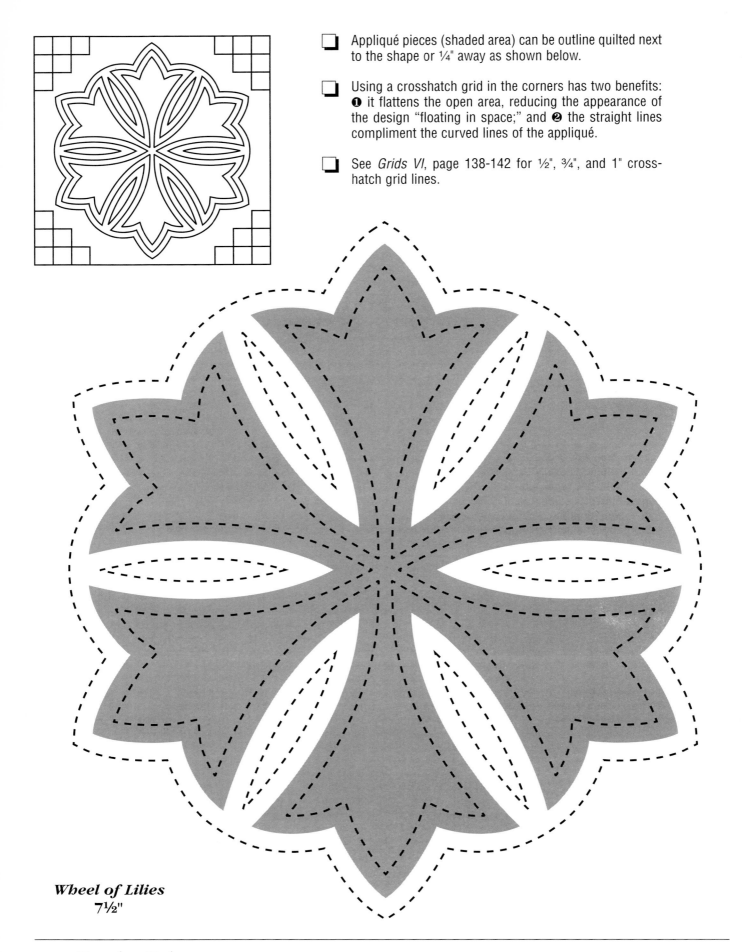

- Appliqué pieces (shaded area) can be outline quilted next to the shape or ¼" away as shown below.

- Using a crosshatch grid in the corners has two benefits: ❶ it flattens the open area, reducing the appearance of the design "floating in space;" and ❷ the straight lines compliment the curved lines of the appliqué.

- See *Grids VI*, page 138-142 for ½", ¾", and 1" crosshatch grid lines.

Wheel of Lilies
7½"

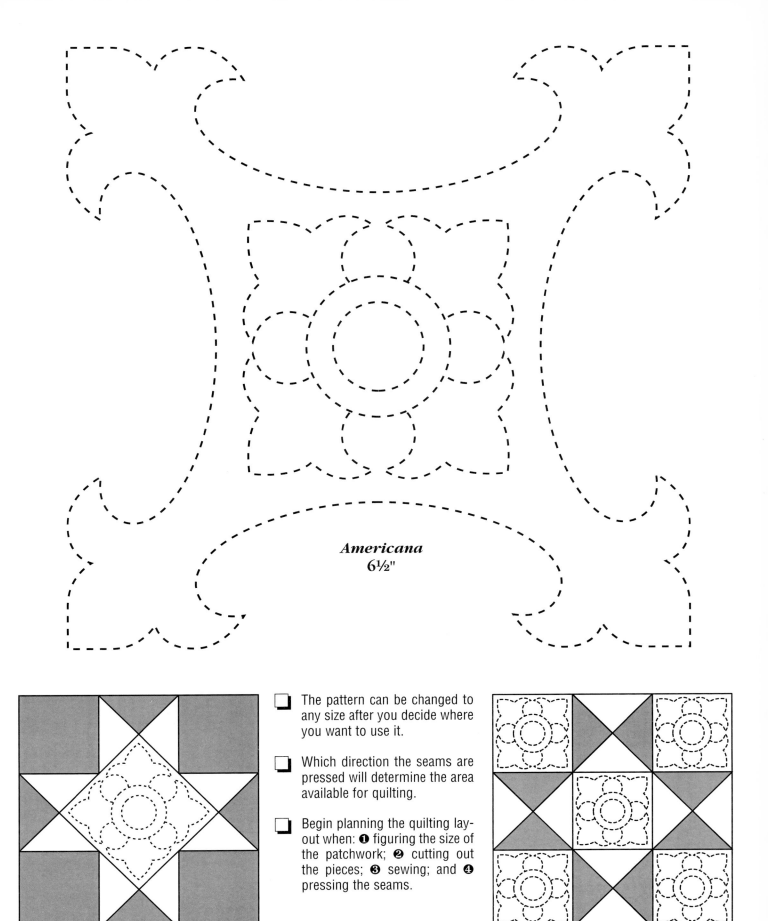

Americana
6½"

The pattern can be changed to any size after you decide where you want to use it.

Which direction the seams are pressed will determine the area available for quilting.

Begin planning the quilting layout when: ❶ figuring the size of the patchwork; ❷ cutting out the pieces; ❸ sewing; and ❹ pressing the seams.

The *Greek Key* is a classic design that works well with a variety of quilting themes and fabric motifs.

Refer to the companion pattern, *Helene*, page 12 and the *Greek Key* border variations it can make.

Four repeats make a 14" circle.

Can be enlarged to any size.

Grecian Sun
14"

By reconnecting the entire pattern (four repeats), you can determine its accuracy and the size that is needed to fit your project.

Make four repeats and connect for the full repeat of the design

Can be enlarged to any size – the bigger the better

Can be quilted by hand or machine

Fanfare 14"

Chapter Three

Sweetheart Designs

- At first glance the designs on the next six pages seem the same. They all have the hearts and tulips motif, yet each has a uniqueness that I will explain.

- *Megan* and *Caroline*, shown here, have different positioning. The first has the motifs placed at 12, 3, 6, and 9 o'clock, the second at 2, 4, 8, and 10 o'clock.

- *Megan's* pattern has two sets of flowers facing in opposite direction. They also touch the edges of the block, locking in the fullness.

- *Caroline's* flowers rotate clockwise and are placed ¼" away from the edges, allowing for any underneath seams.

- A silhouette stencil is a marking tool used to transfer or trace the quilting pattern onto fabric.

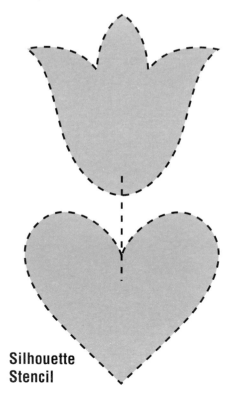

Silhouette Stencil

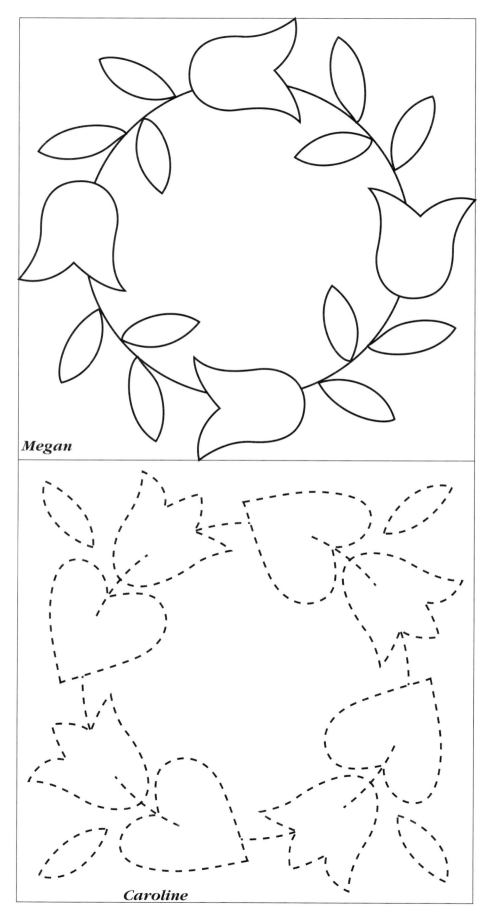

Megan

Caroline

*Copy the design and connect
two repeats to make the wreath.
Extra tulips can be added*

**Judi's Left-Handed
Tulip Wreath
12"**

Placement Diagram

Silhouette Stencil

A common concern with quilting patterns is that the space, or area, is completely filled. This is accomplished by combining the main design with background stitches. Meandering lines and grids are obvious choices, but first consider enlarging the design.

Notice how the four blocks of *Lindajean's Garden* in the placement diagram above are connected with the tulips touching the seam lines. Even the hearts in the corner of the blocks converge to form a new shape in the middle.

- Quilting patterns make great appliqué patterns, too! Try the Shadow Appliqué technique where the shapes are cut without seams and fused, or spray basted in place. A layer of sheer fabric is placed on top and the entire sandwich is then outline quilted.

- Make extra copies and reconnect any patterns that have been separated into quarters *before* you use it. Check for accuracy and decide on any adjustments.

Lindajean's Garden
9½"

Placement Diagram

Using multiple repeats is a very effective quilting technique. Keep in mind what happens at the corners. Do they march off the edge? Miter? Reverse or rotate? These are choices easily made when you have extra copies of the design to play with.

To vary the basic design motif, the hearts and flowers were mitered in *Tulip Patch Border,* shown on the next page, and placed with the tulips almost touching.

The design was then modified into a continuous line pattern and placed in the corners to form a new block.

Julie's Tulip Border
2¾"

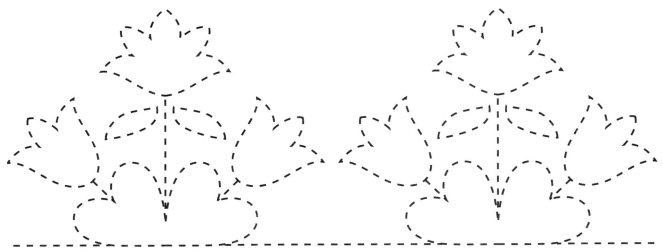

Tulip Patch Border

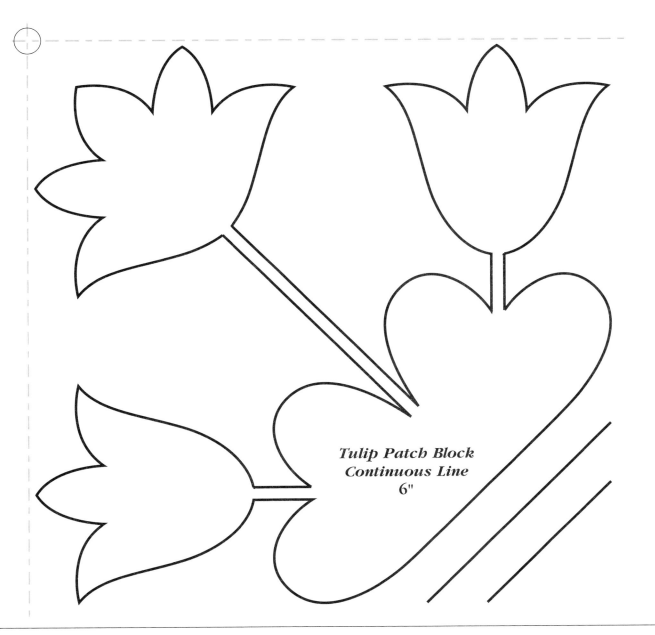

Tulip Patch Block
Continuous Line
6"

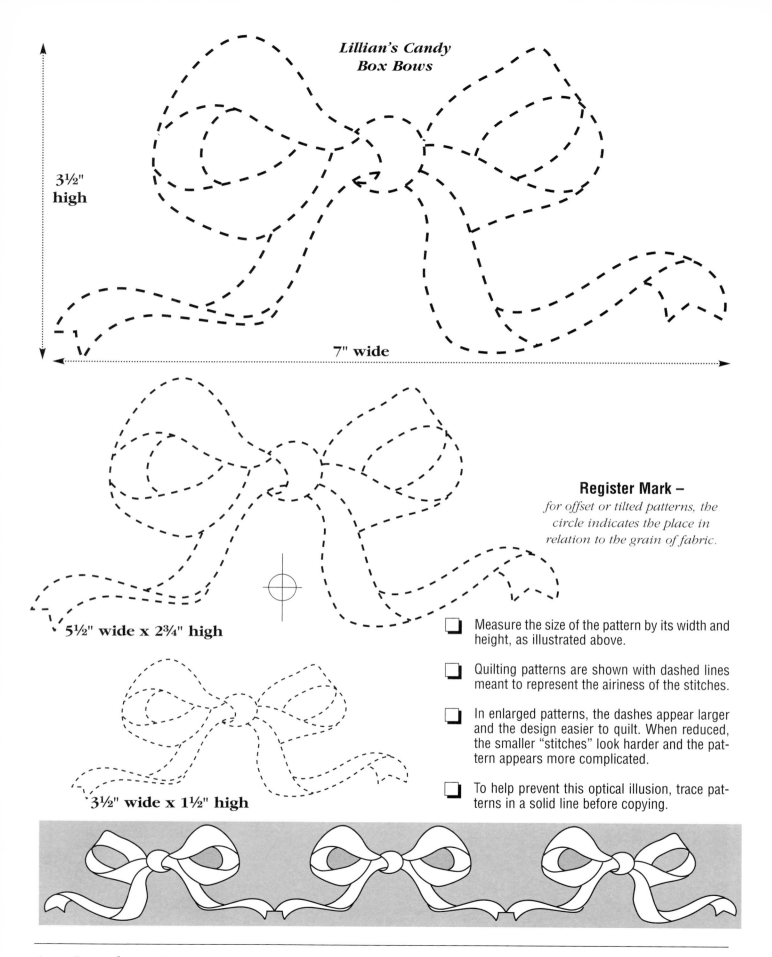

Lillian's Candy Box Bows

3½" high

7" wide

5½" wide x 2¾" high

Register Mark –

for offset or tilted patterns, the circle indicates the place in relation to the grain of fabric.

☐ Measure the size of the pattern by its width and height, as illustrated above.

☐ Quilting patterns are shown with dashed lines meant to represent the airiness of the stitches.

☐ In enlarged patterns, the dashes appear larger and the design easier to quilt. When reduced, the smaller "stitches" look harder and the pattern appears more complicated.

☐ To help prevent this optical illusion, trace patterns in a solid line before copying.

3½" wide x 1½" high

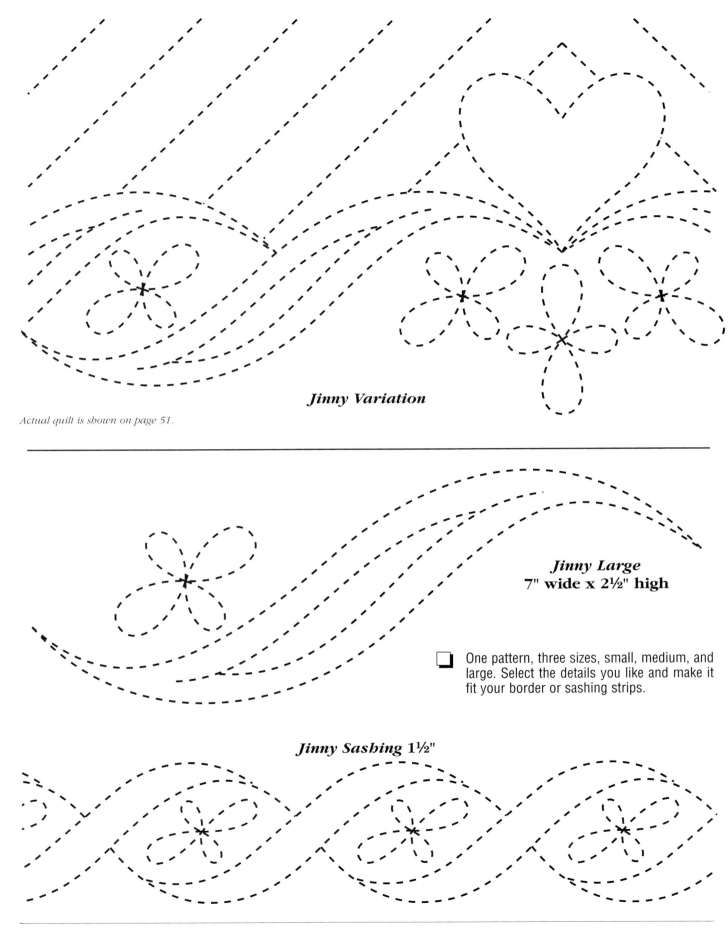

Jinny Variation

Actual quilt is shown on page 51.

Jinny Large
7" wide x 2½" high

⬜ One pattern, three sizes, small, medium, and large. Select the details you like and make it fit your border or sashing strips.

Jinny Sashing 1½"

detail from
Climbing Clematis

Climbing Clematis

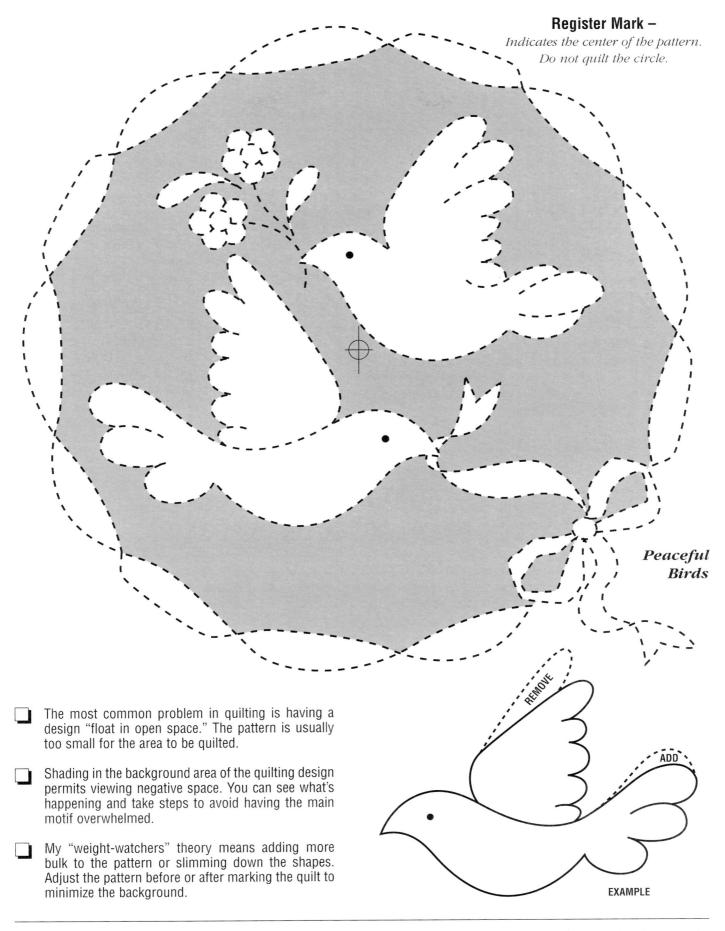

Peaceful
Birds

REMOVE

ADD

EXAMPLE

☐ The most common problem in quilting is having a design "float in open space." The pattern is usually too small for the area to be quilted.

☐ Shading in the background area of the quilting design permits viewing negative space. You can see what's happening and take steps to avoid having the main motif overwhelmed.

☐ My "weight-watchers" theory means adding more bulk to the pattern or slimming down the shapes. Adjust the pattern before or after marking the quilt to minimize the background.

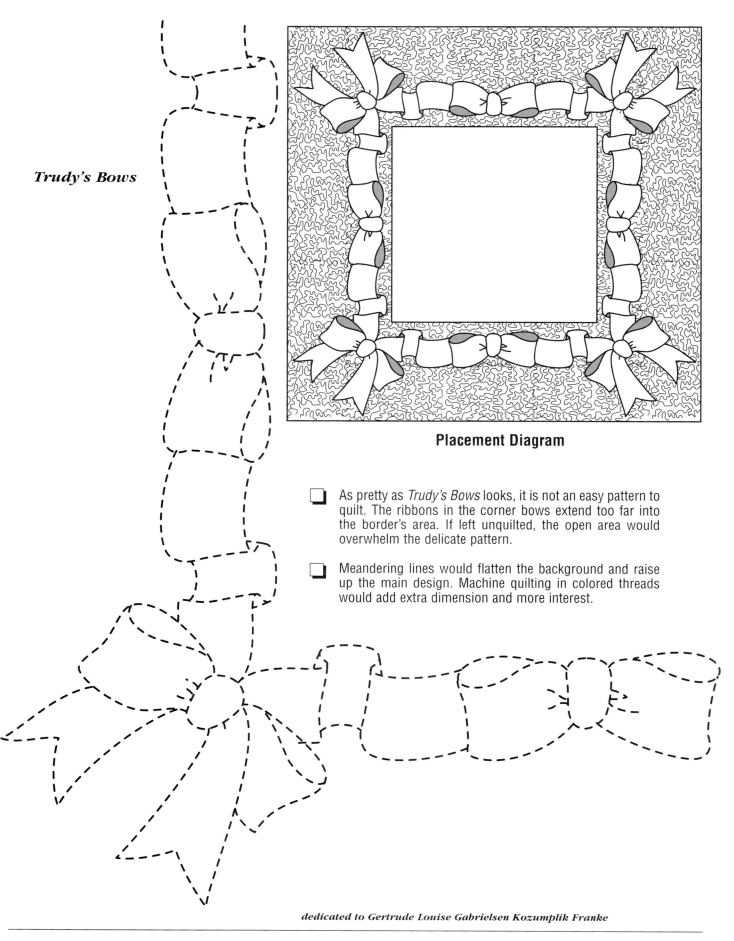

Trudy's Bows

Placement Diagram

As pretty as *Trudy's Bows* looks, it is not an easy pattern to quilt. The ribbons in the corner bows extend too far into the border's area. If left unquilted, the open area would overwhelm the delicate pattern.

Meandering lines would flatten the background and raise up the main design. Machine quilting in colored threads would add extra dimension and more interest.

dedicated to Gertrude Louise Gabrielsen Kozumplik Franke

Placement Diagram: Enlarge to desired size. Simplify details and add trimmings.

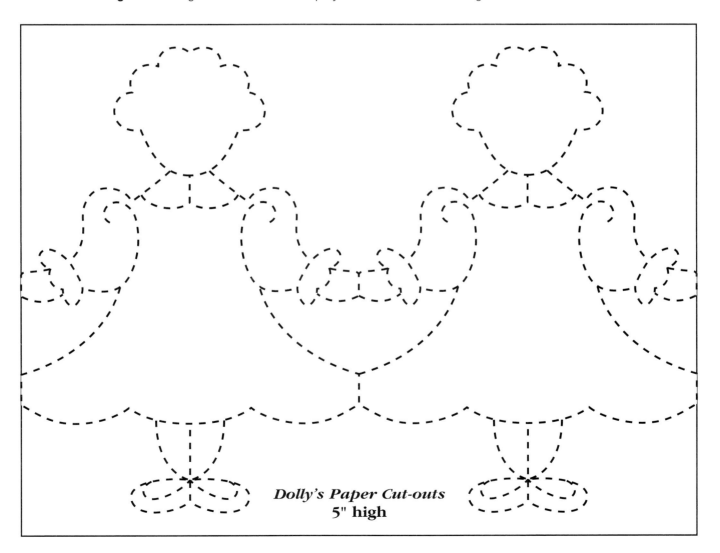

Dolly's Paper Cut-outs
5" high

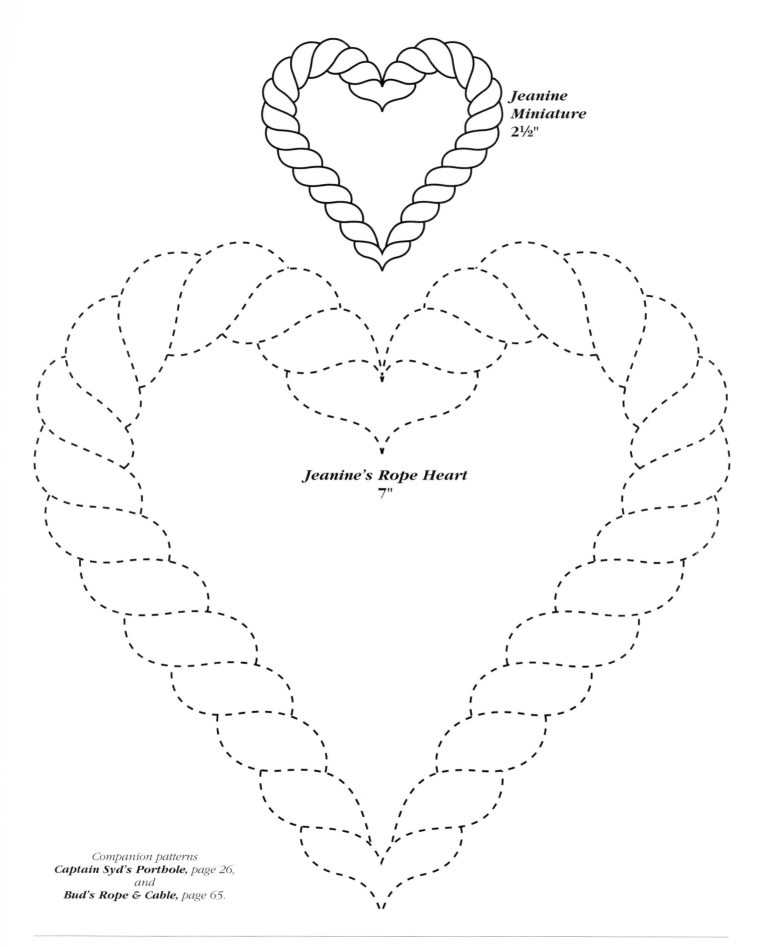

Jeanine Miniature
2½"

Jeanine's Rope Heart
7"

Companion patterns
Captain Syd's Porthole, *page 26,*
and
Bud's Rope & Cable, *page 65.*

Helen's Copy & Use Quilting Patterns – Helen Squire

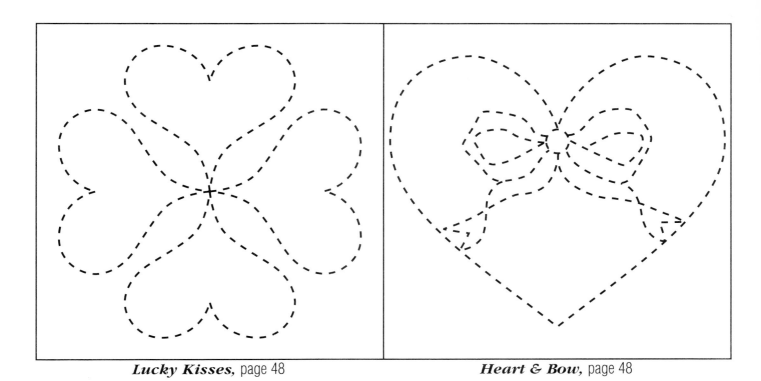

Lucky Kisses, page 48   **Heart & Bow,** page 48

Embossed Heart, page 49   **Entwined Hearts,** page 49

Philodendron
Sashing 2"

Lucky Kisses
4½"

Heart & Bow
4½"

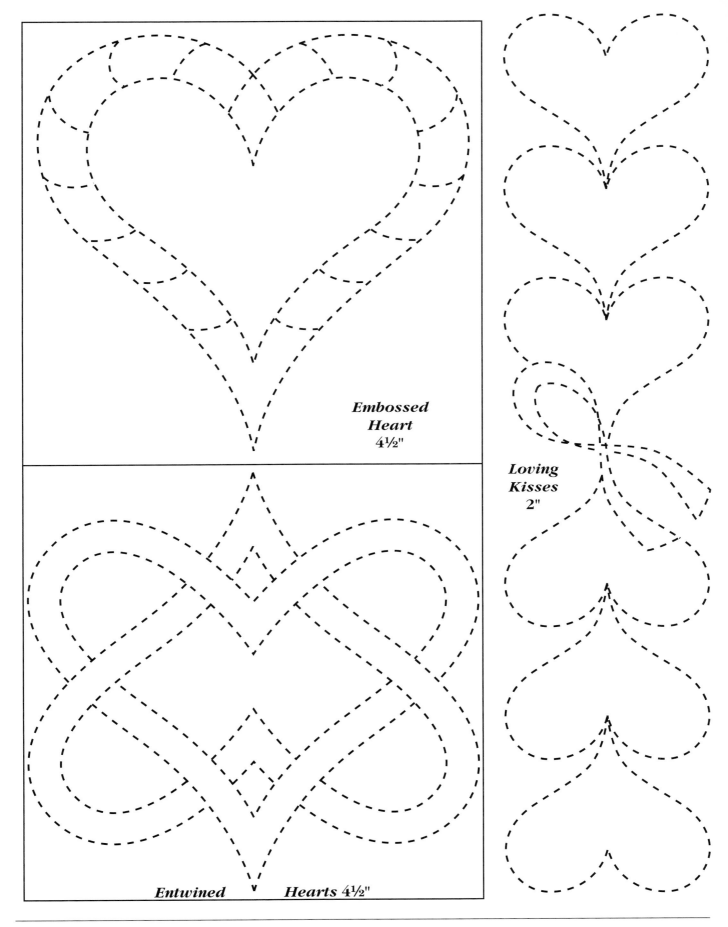

*Embossed
Heart*
4½"

*Loving
Kisses*
2"

Entwined *Hearts* 4½"

My Heart Belongs to Baby

Companion pattern
Jinny,
page 41.

Making a Muslin Master of the Quilting Design Layout

☐ Instead of sheets of paper, create a master pattern drawn on muslin. It's durable, easy to fold, does not rip, and is cheaper than large-sized paper! It can be used again and again.

☐ Design and plan for one-quarter of the layout plus a two-inch overlap which allows you to see if the pattern is to be flipped, flopped, rotated, mitered at corners, or reversed at the center of the quilt, etc.

☐ Draw the quilting design on the muslin with a fine-line indelible black marker. Pin light-colored quilt fabric on top of the muslin. Trace the entire design with a regular color-matched chalk pencil.

photo by Myron Miller

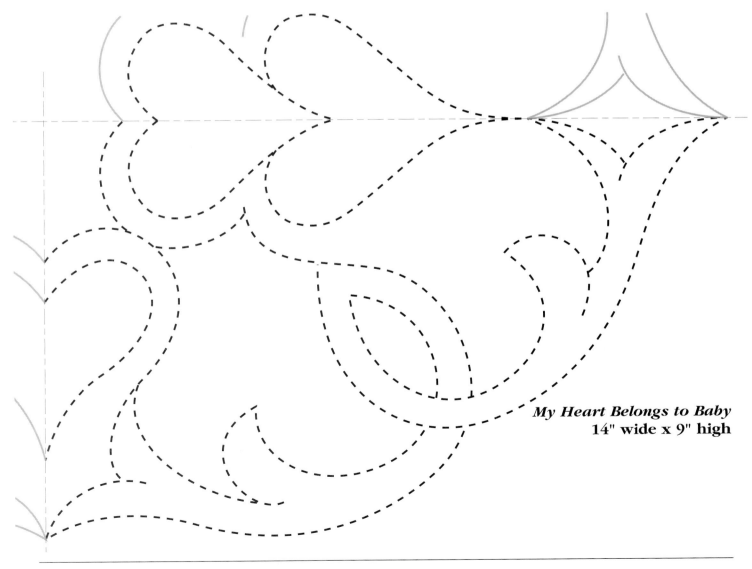

My Heart Belongs to Baby
14" wide x 9" high

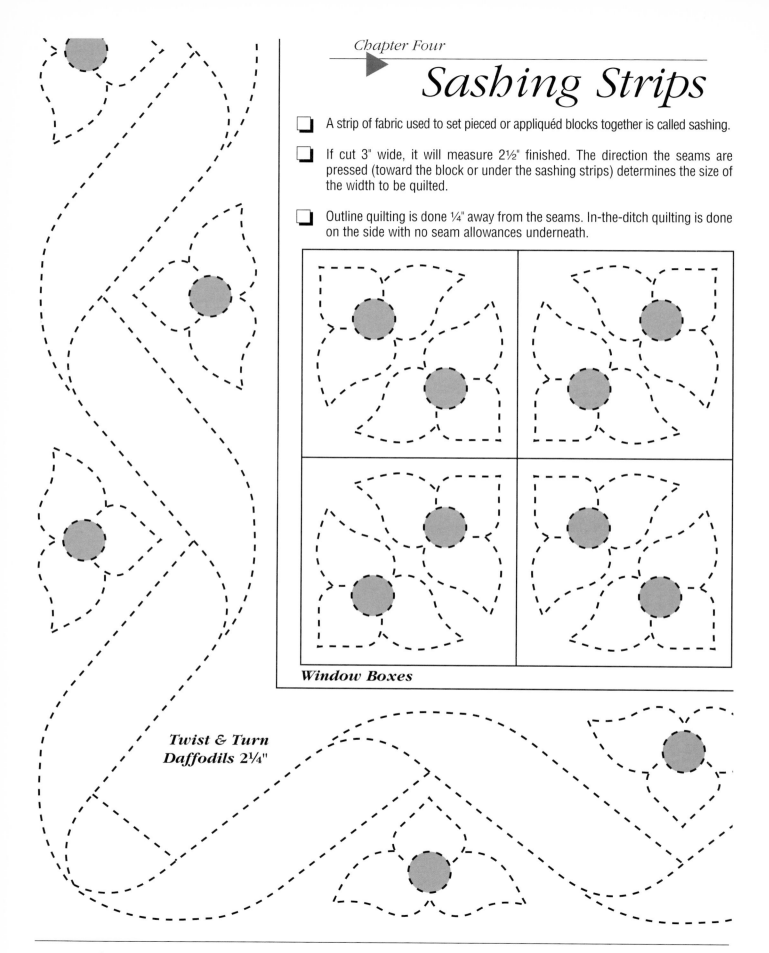

Chapter Four

Sashing Strips

A strip of fabric used to set pieced or appliquéd blocks together is called sashing.

If cut 3" wide, it will measure 2½" finished. The direction the seams are pressed (toward the block or under the sashing strips) determines the size of the width to be quilted.

Outline quilting is done ¼" away from the seams. In-the-ditch quilting is done on the side with no seam allowances underneath.

Window Boxes

Twist & Turn Daffodils 2¼"

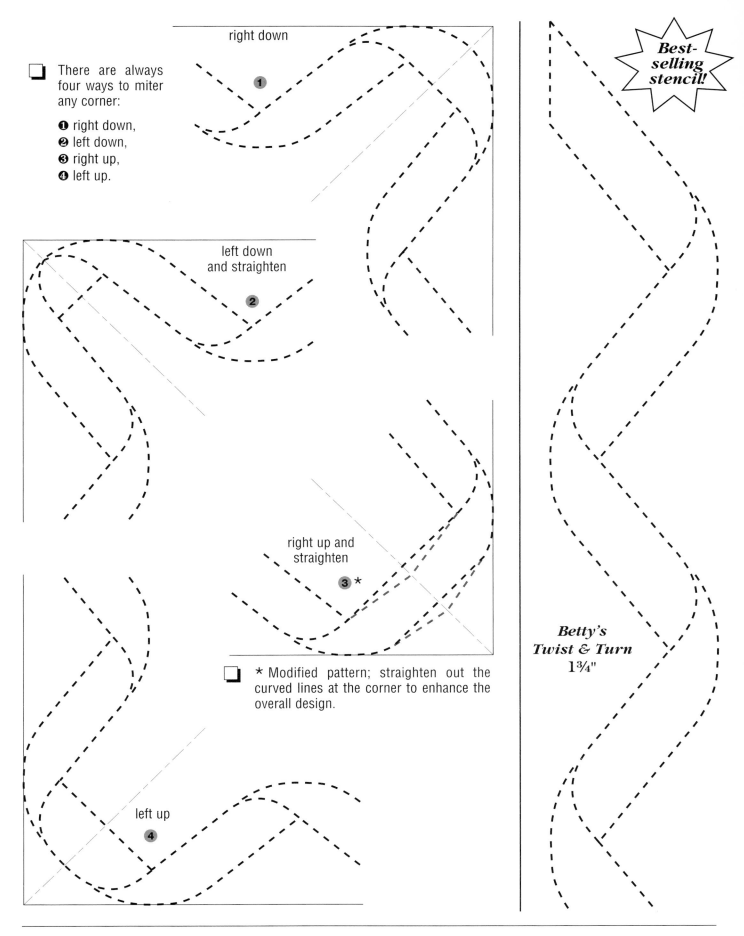

There are always four ways to miter any corner:

❶ right down,
❷ left down,
❸ right up,
❹ left up.

right down

❶

left down and straighten

❷

right up and straighten

❸ *

* Modified pattern; straighten out the curved lines at the corner to enhance the overall design.

left up

❹

Best-selling stencil!

Betty's
Twist & Turn
1¾"

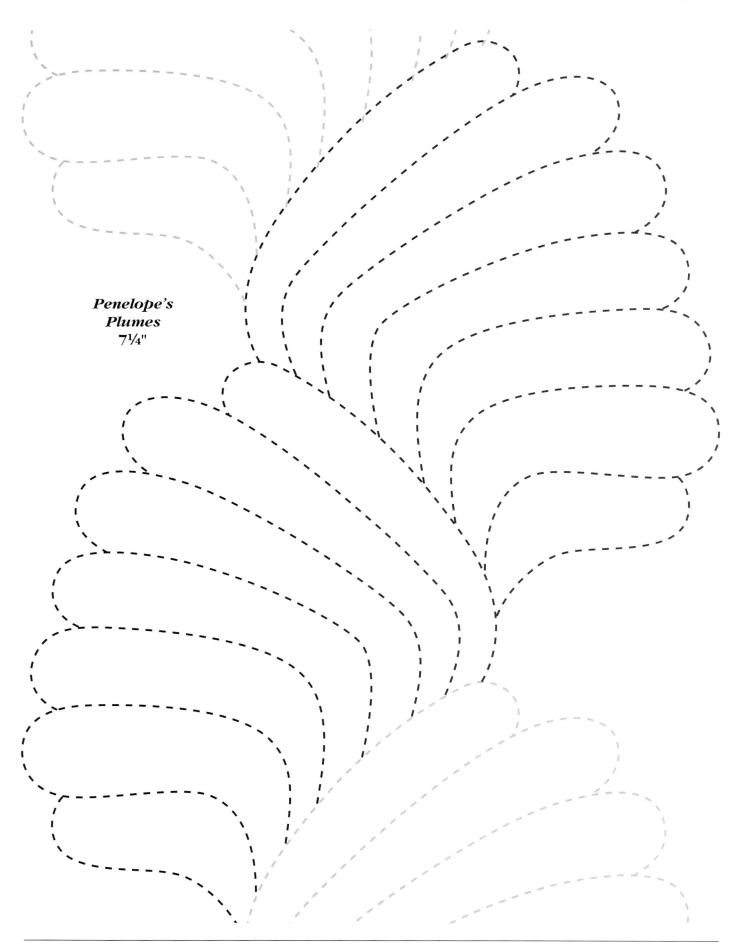

Penelope's
Plumes
7¼"

Placement Diagram

Penelope's Plumes 4"

Stella's Delight 4"

Register Mark –
*Helps keep the pattern
straight. When copying
repeats, match the circles.*

Pumpkin Seed 2½"

Caroline's Lattice
3½"

Caroline's Lattice
2¼"

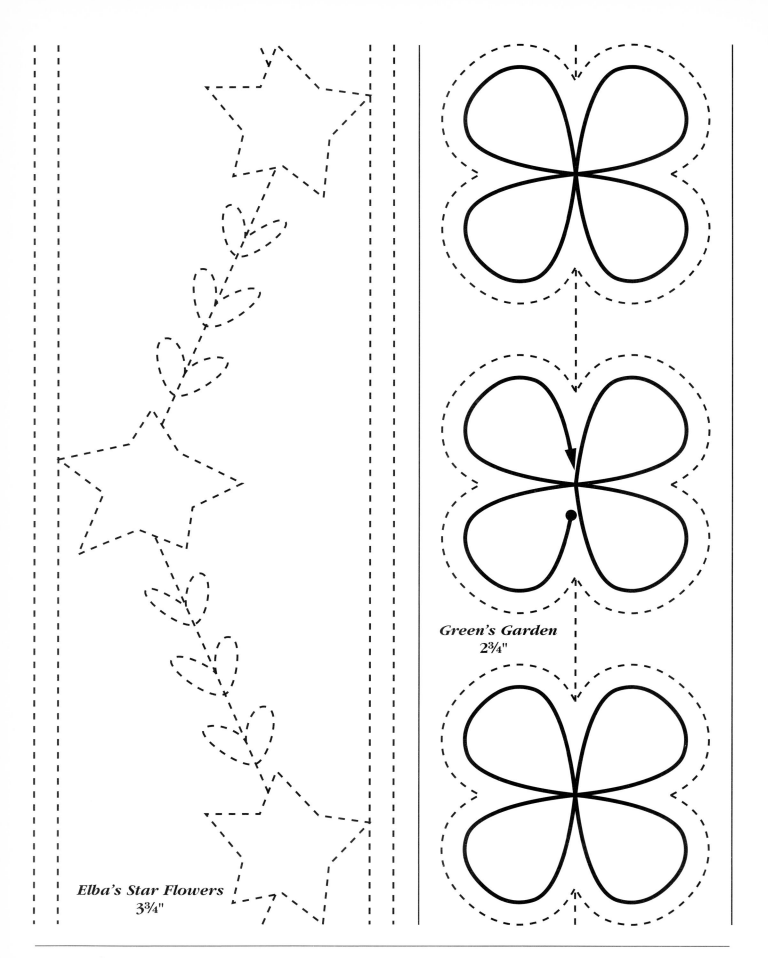

Green's Garden
2¾"

Elba's Star Flowers
3¾"

Frank's Flower
4½"

2¼"

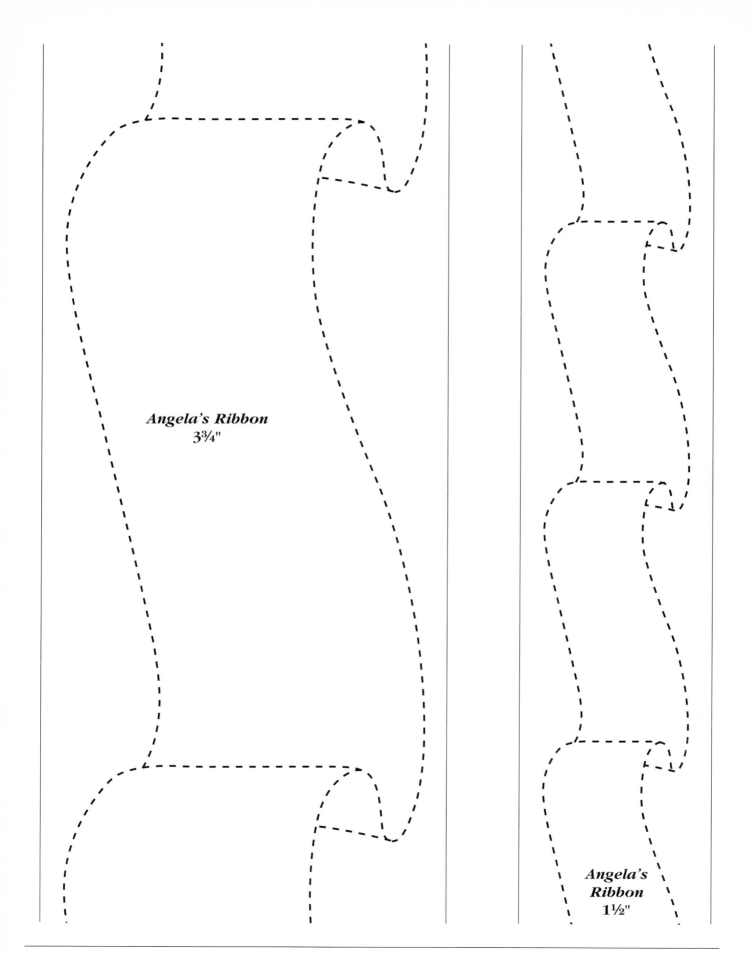

Angela's Ribbon
3¾"

Angela's Ribbon
1½"

Elisa's Posies and Grid 3½"

Helen's Copy & Use Quilting Patterns – Helen Squire

Placement Diagram

Aimee's Chain
1½"

Bab's Berries
1½"

Double Feather Border
3¾"

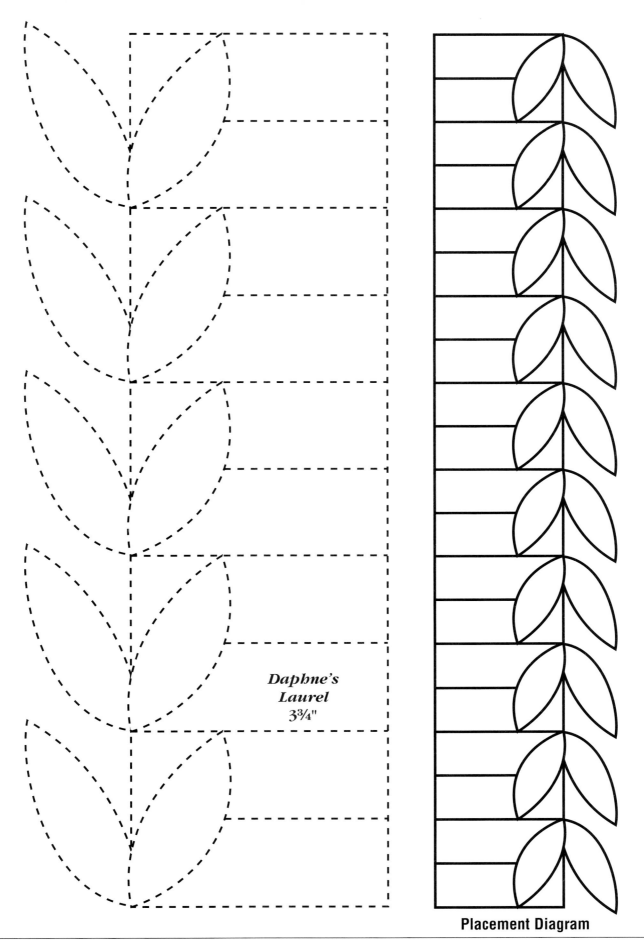

*Daphne's
Laurel*
3¾"

Placement Diagram

Chapter Five

Borders & Blocks

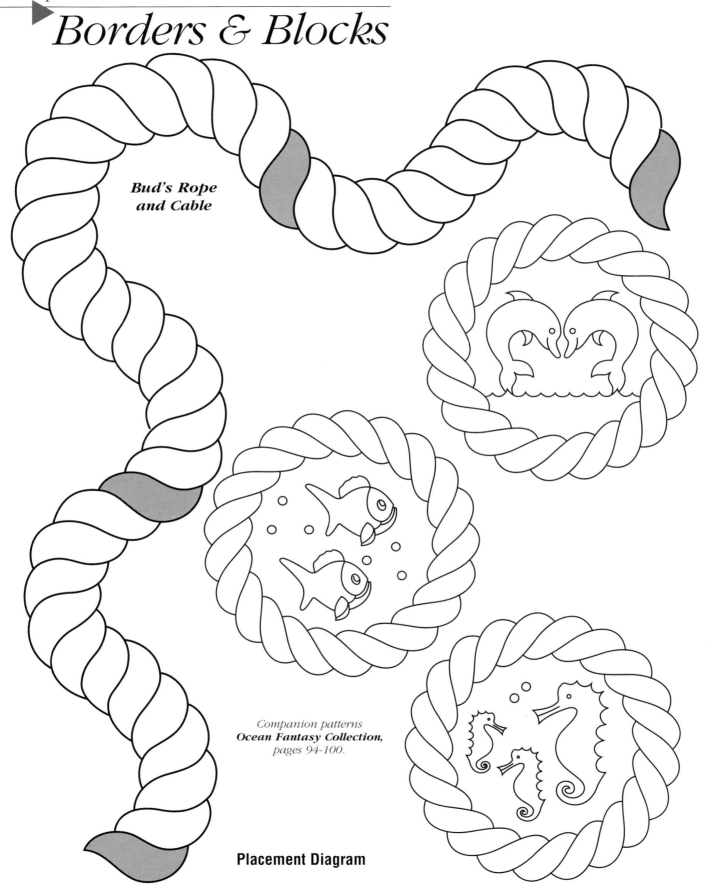

**Bud's Rope
and Cable**

Companion patterns
Ocean Fantasy Collection,
pages 94-100.

Placement Diagram

Bud's Rope and Cable

Companion patterns include
Captain Syd's Porthole, *page 26, and*
Jeanine's Rope Heart, *page 46.*

*Overlap darkened areas
to connect pattern*

Carla's Conch 2¾"

Carla's Conch 1¾"

Reversed

Helen's Copy & Use Quilting Patterns – Helen Squire

Version 1

Version 2

Version 3

Version 4

reverse
at center

Carla's Conch Variations

Pattern can be enlarged to any size

1 To make a wider border pattern, use two copies of *Carla's Conch*, page 66, one reversed and flopped.

2 Layer copies facing together and staple securely along the longer edge. Final designs depend on whether they are connected on the top or bottom of the pattern.

3 Slide the pattern down until the design is appealing to you. Finger crease the fold and redraw an accurate copy. Refer to illustrations on page 8 for mitering corners.

4 Omit any small details to better emphasize the flow. Use this new pattern to create a companion design, *Lynda's Heart Block*.

Carla's Corner Variation

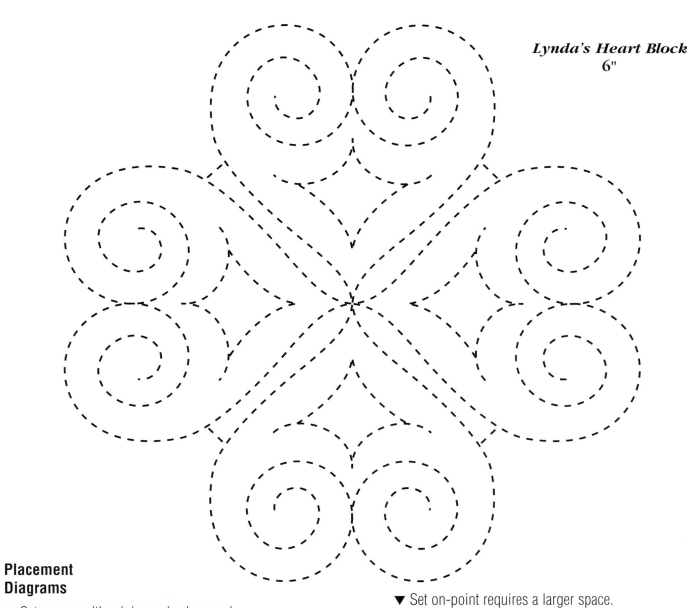

Placement Diagrams

▼ Set square with minimum background.

▼ Set on-point requires a larger space.

Placement Diagram

Can be quilted by hand or machine

Ocotillo's Border
4"

Fred's Maze
2"

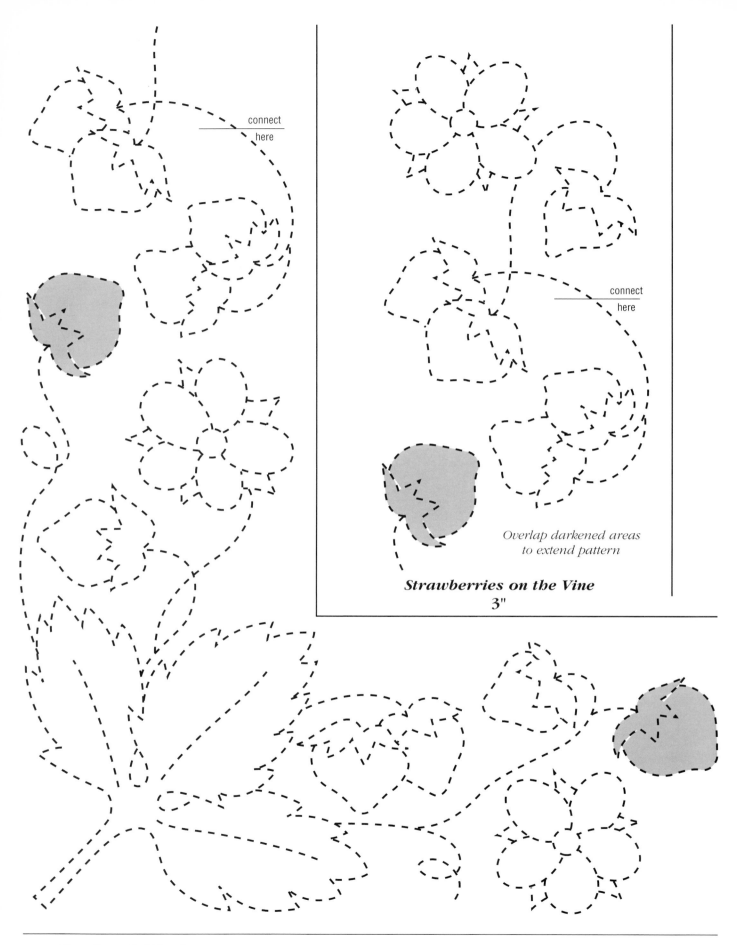

connect
here

connect
here

*Overlap darkened areas
to extend pattern*

Strawberries on the Vine
3"

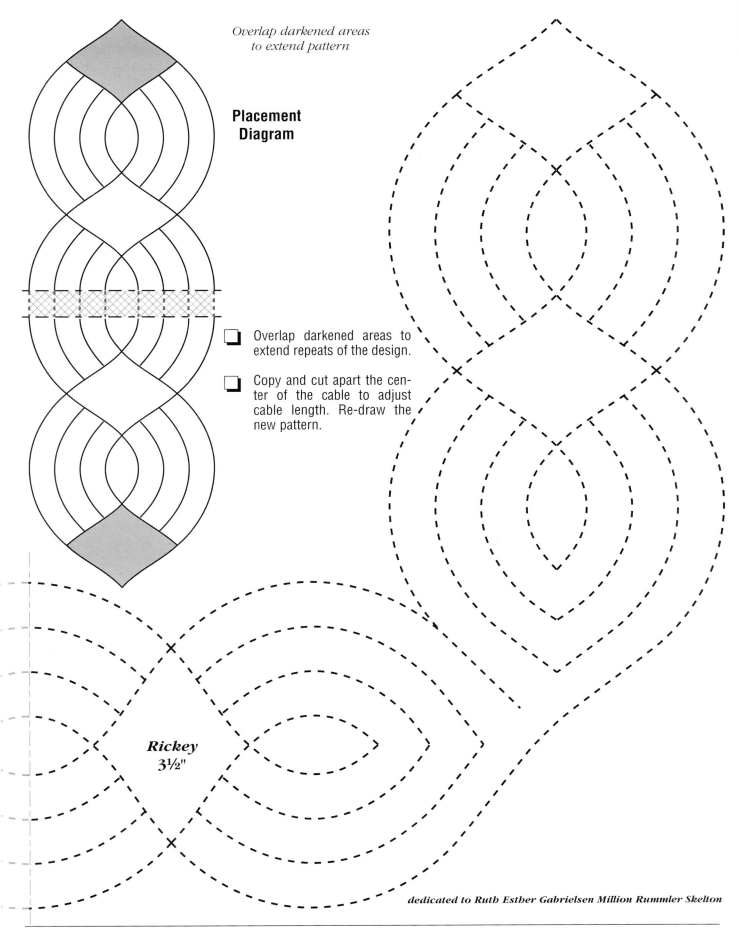

*Overlap darkened areas
to extend pattern*

**Placement
Diagram**

☐ Overlap darkened areas to extend repeats of the design.

☐ Copy and cut apart the center of the cable to adjust cable length. Re-draw the new pattern.

Rickey
3½"

dedicated to Ruth Esther Gabrielsen Million Rummler Skelton

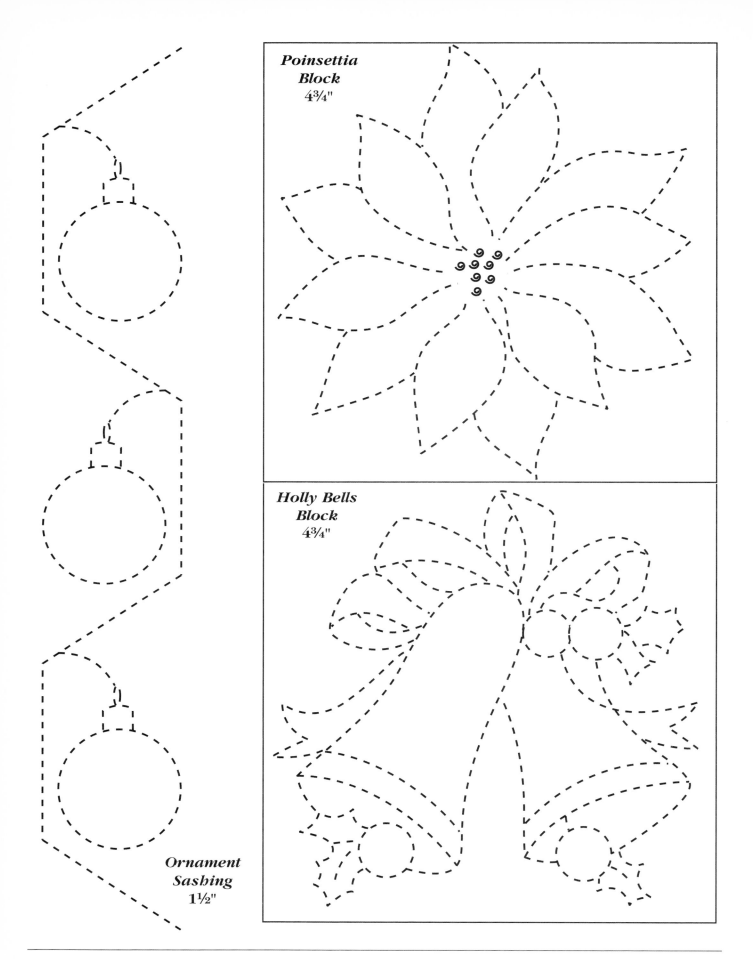

Poinsettia Block 4¾"

Holly Bells Block 4¾"

Ornament Sashing 1½"

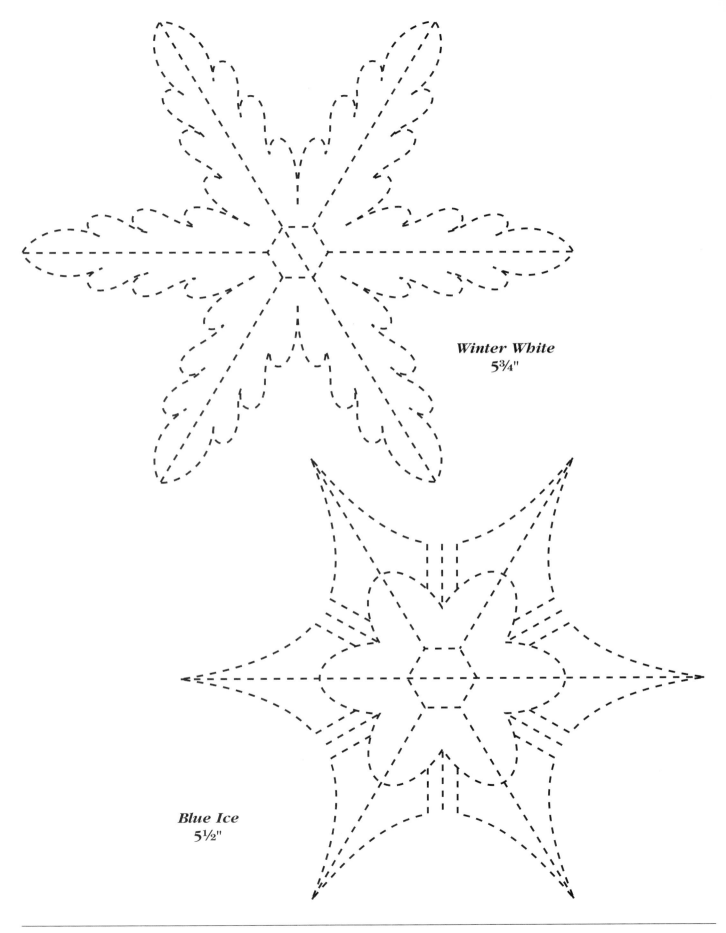

Winter White
5¾"

Blue Ice
5½"

- [ ] A good way to anchor a variety of designs is to add a straight double-line border behind the motifs.

- [ ] Reposition or re-draw the design's shape (poinsettia petal) to prevent curves and points from running into the straight line.

Placement Diagram

connect here

Holiday Border
5½"

connect here

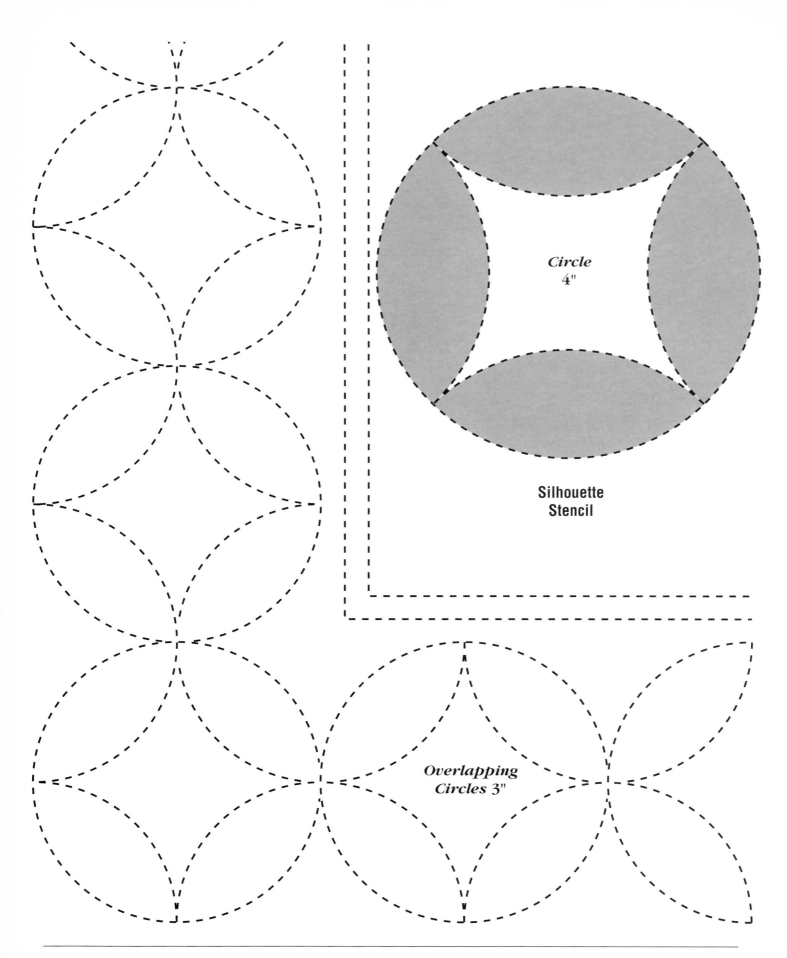

*Circle
4"*

**Silhouette
Stencil**

*Overlapping
Circles 3"*

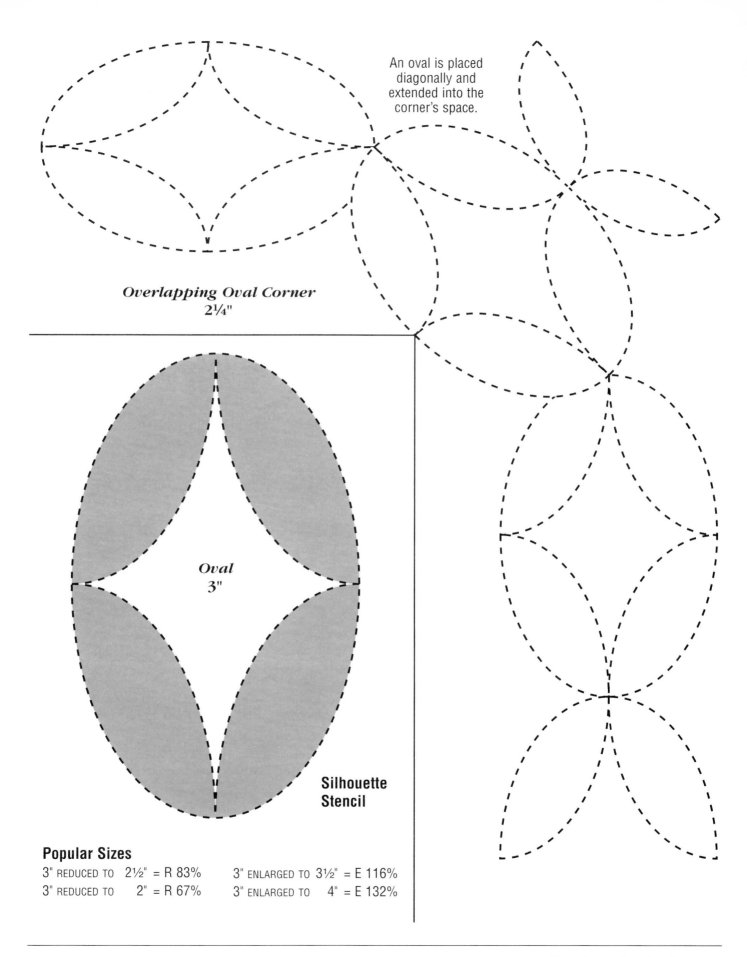

An oval is placed
diagonally and
extended into the
corner's space.

Overlapping Oval Corner
2¼"

Oval
3"

Silhouette Stencil

Popular Sizes

3" REDUCED TO   2½" = R 83%   3" ENLARGED TO 3½" = E 116%
3" REDUCED TO   2" = R 67%   3" ENLARGED TO   4" = E 132%

connect here

Viola's Vine **2**
3½"

Viola's Vine **1**
3½"

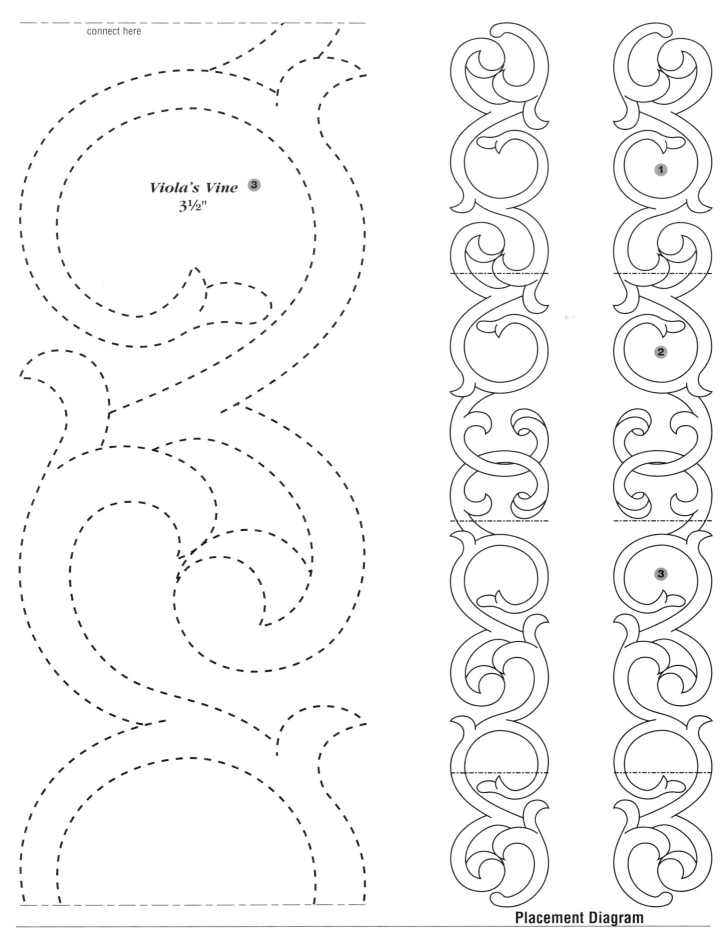

connect here

Viola's Vine **3**
3½"

Placement Diagram

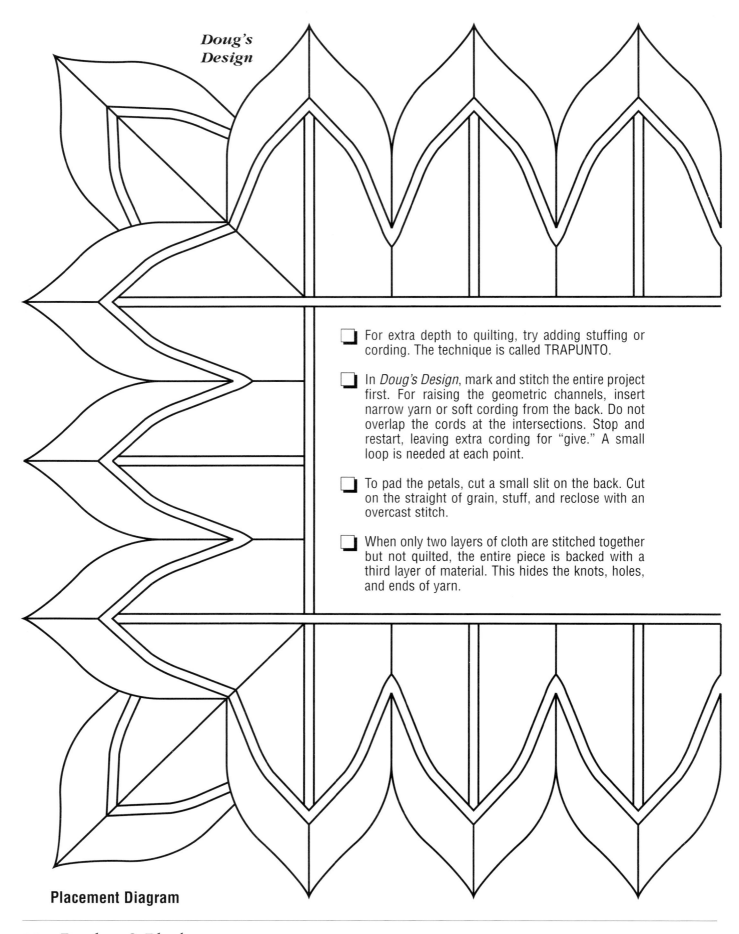

Doug's Design

For extra depth to quilting, try adding stuffing or cording. The technique is called TRAPUNTO.

In *Doug's Design*, mark and stitch the entire project first. For raising the geometric channels, insert narrow yarn or soft cording from the back. Do not overlap the cords at the intersections. Stop and restart, leaving extra cording for "give." A small loop is needed at each point.

To pad the petals, cut a small slit on the back. Cut on the straight of grain, stuff, and reclose with an overcast stitch.

When only two layers of cloth are stitched together but not quilted, the entire piece is backed with a third layer of material. This hides the knots, holes, and ends of yarn.

Placement Diagram

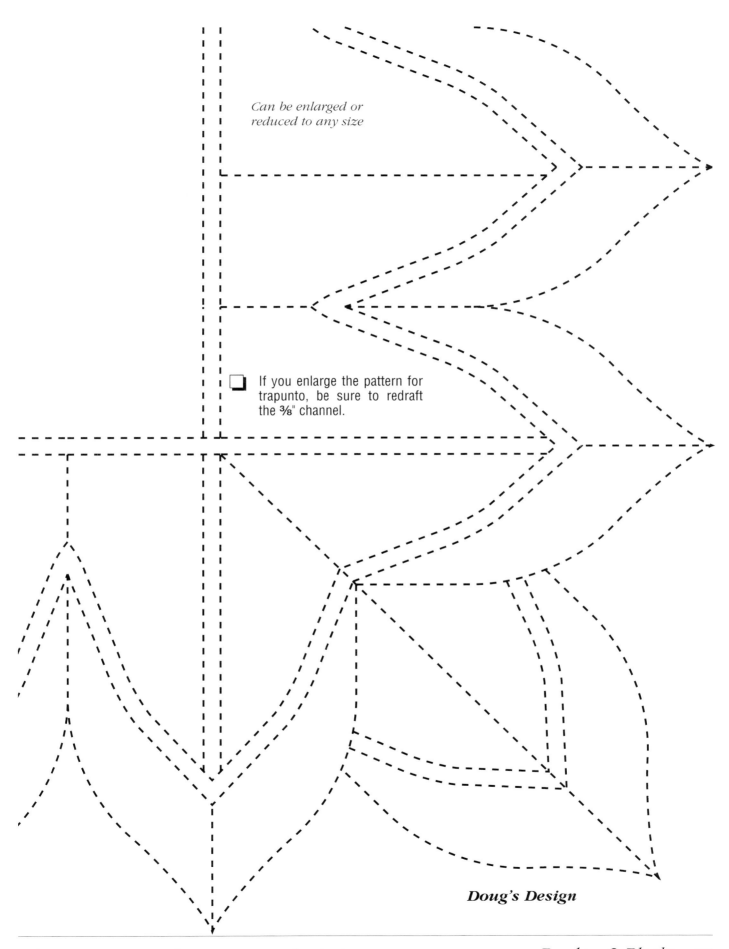

Can be enlarged or reduced to any size

If you enlarge the pattern for trapunto, be sure to redraft the ⅜" channel.

Doug's Design

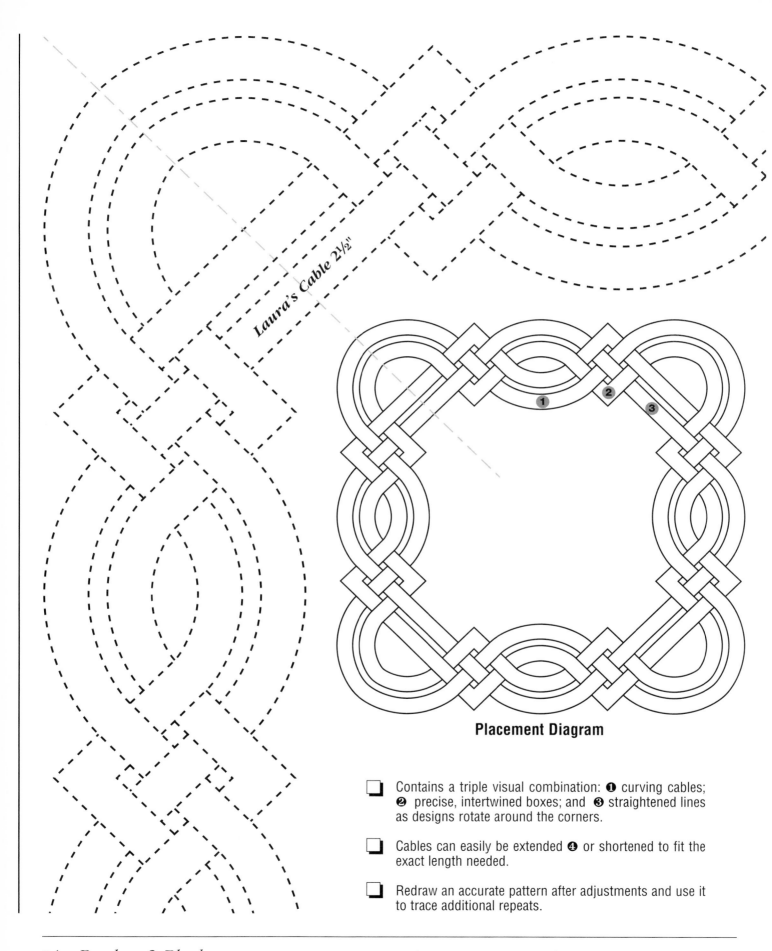

Laura's Cable 2½"

Placement Diagram

Contains a triple visual combination: ❶ curving cables; ❷ precise, intertwined boxes; and ❸ straightened lines as designs rotate around the corners.

Cables can easily be extended ❹ or shortened to fit the exact length needed.

Redraw an accurate pattern after adjustments and use it to trace additional repeats.

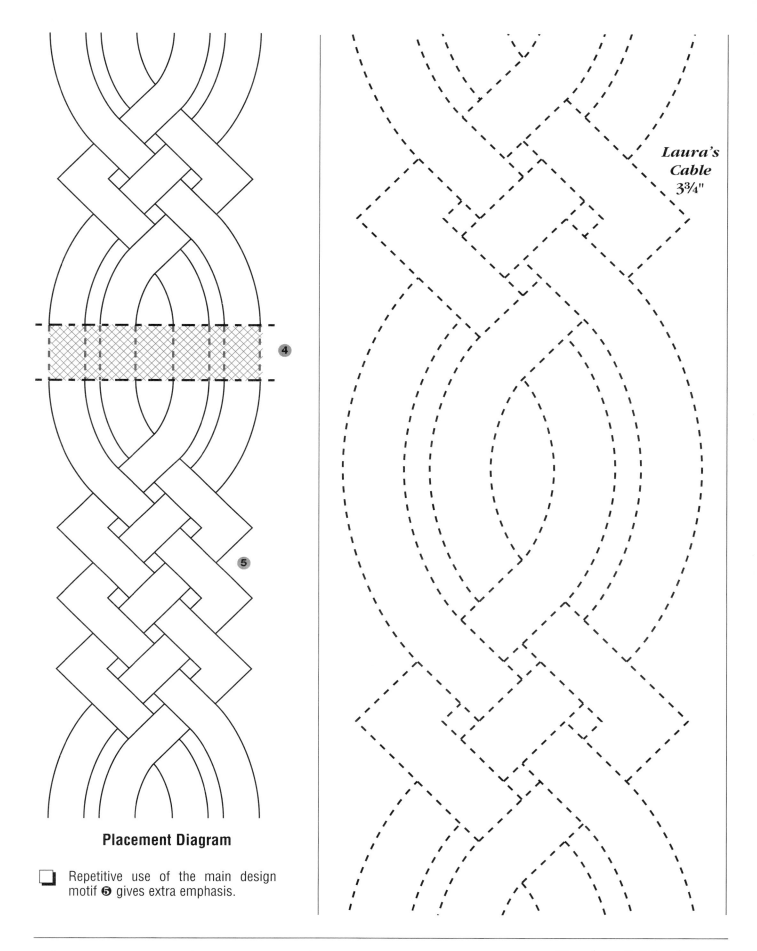

Laura's Cable 3¾"

Placement Diagram

Repetitive use of the main design motif ❺ gives extra emphasis.

Placement Diagram: Pattern can be reversed at center ✱ or at equal intervals along the border.

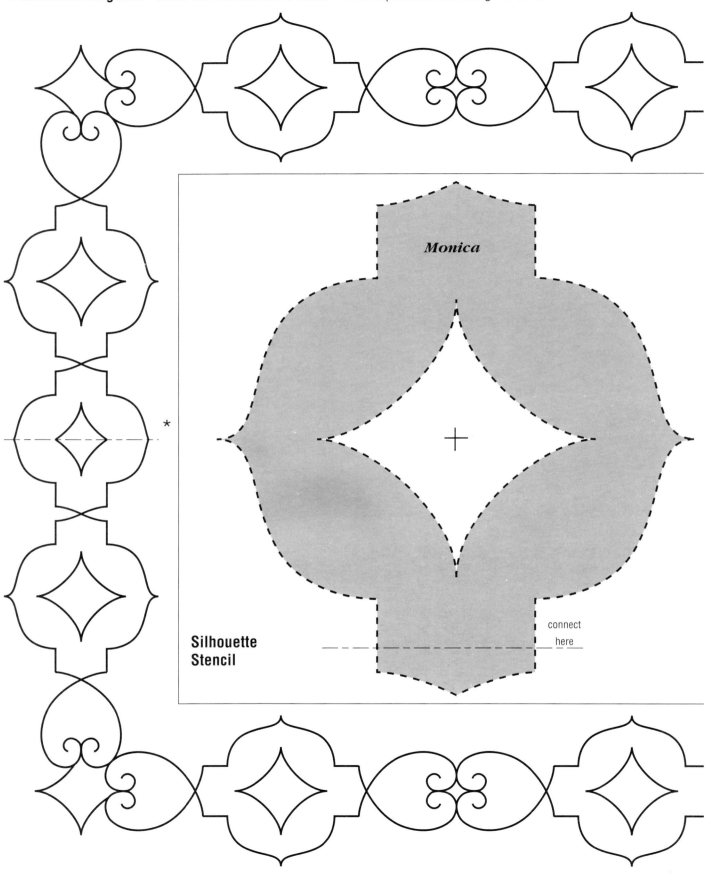

Monica

✱

Silhouette Stencil

connect
here

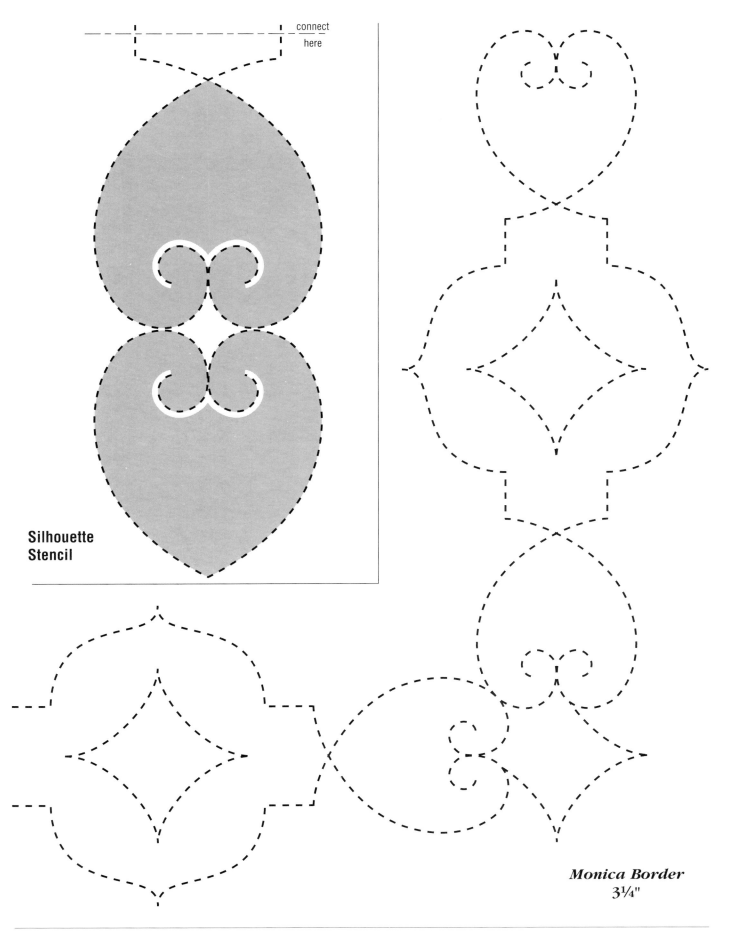

connect
here

**Silhouette
Stencil**

Monica Border
3¼"

Chapter Six

Fun Patterns

Michael's Circus Tent
7½" wide x 8½" high

Helen's Copy & Use Quilting Patterns – Helen Squire

Teddy Bear, page 90   **Panda,** page 91

Lion Cub, page 92   **Tiger Cub,** page 93

To make a pattern fit in an 8" wide x 10" high area using *Teddy Bear*, page 90:

7" W x 9" H @ 111% = 7¾" W   x   10" H

7" W x 9" H @ 114% =   8" W   x   10¼" H

7" W x 9" H @ 108% = 7½" W   x   9¾" H

Both measurements are needed, then compromise the difference. To reduce for a 5" x 7" block:

7" W x 9" H @ 78% = 5½" W   x   7" H

7" W x 9" H @ 72% =   5" W   x   6½" H

7" W x 9" H @ 70% = 4⅞" W   x   6¼" H

Teddy Bear
7" wide x 9" high
without box

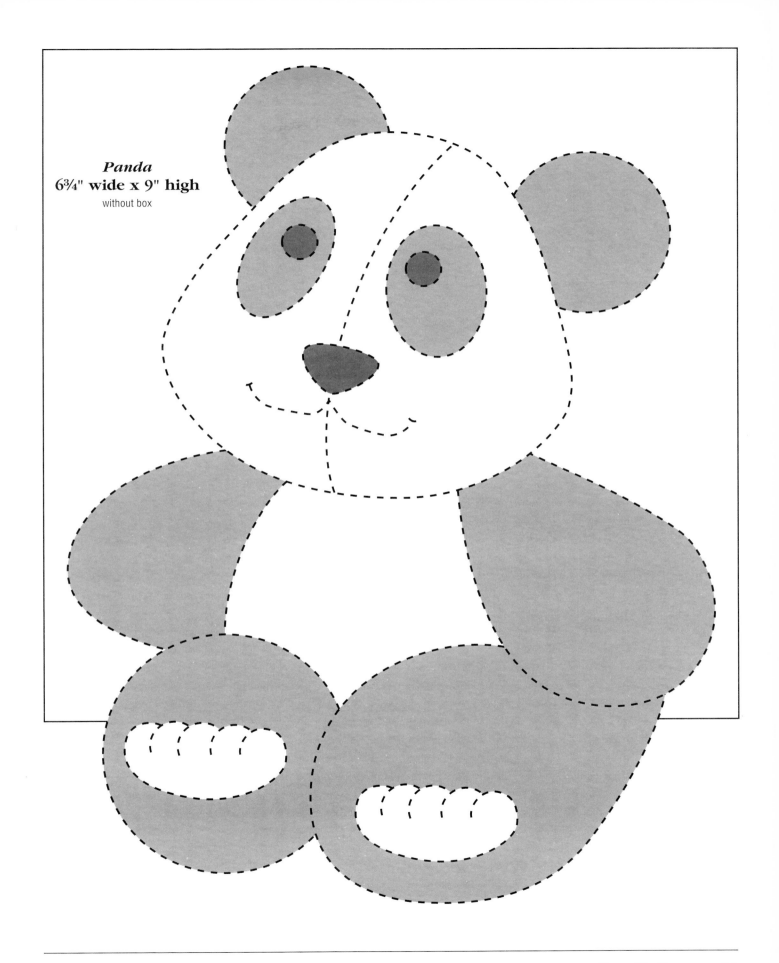

Panda
6¾" wide x 9" high
without box

Lion Cub
6½" wide x 8¾" high
without box

Tiger Cub
6¼" wide x 8½" high
without box

**Seahorse
7¾" wide x 9½" high**

2½" wide x 4" high

When reducing designs, simplify details. Notice that the back of large seahorse has nine spikes, and the small one has only eight

Placement Diagram: This pattern looks awesome when done in Hawaiian appliqué!

Ocean Fantasy Collection

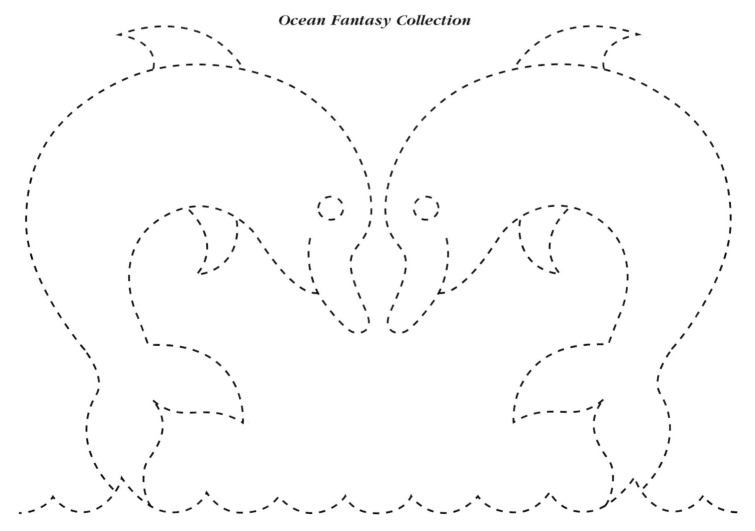

Dancing Dolphins
7½" wide x 5¼" high

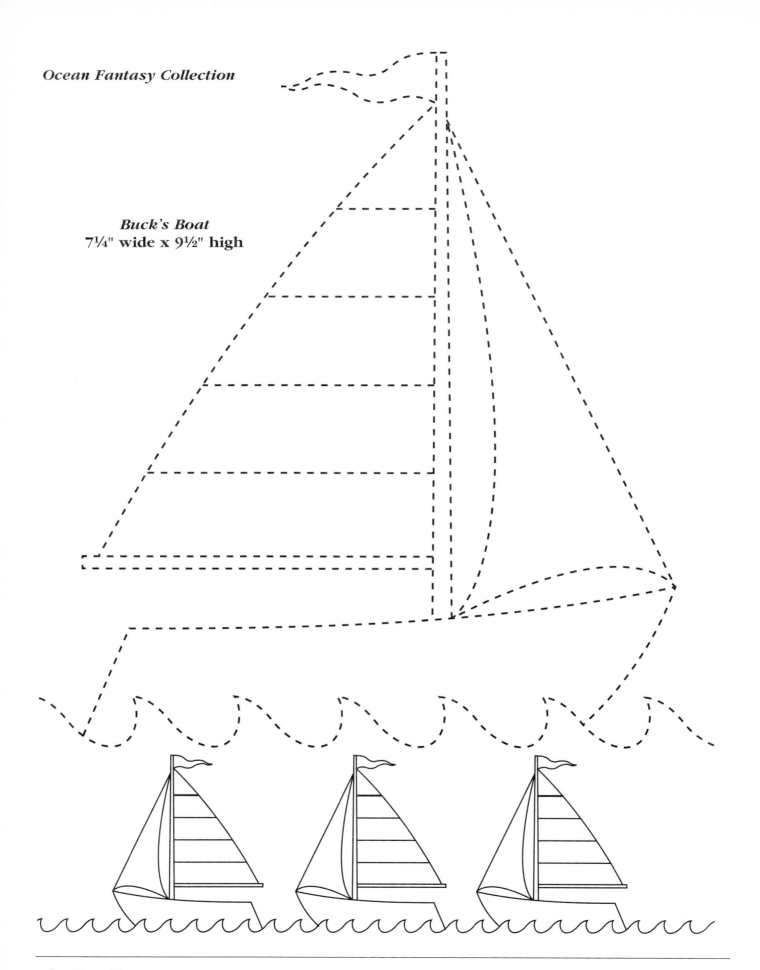

Buck's Boat
7¼" wide x 9½" high

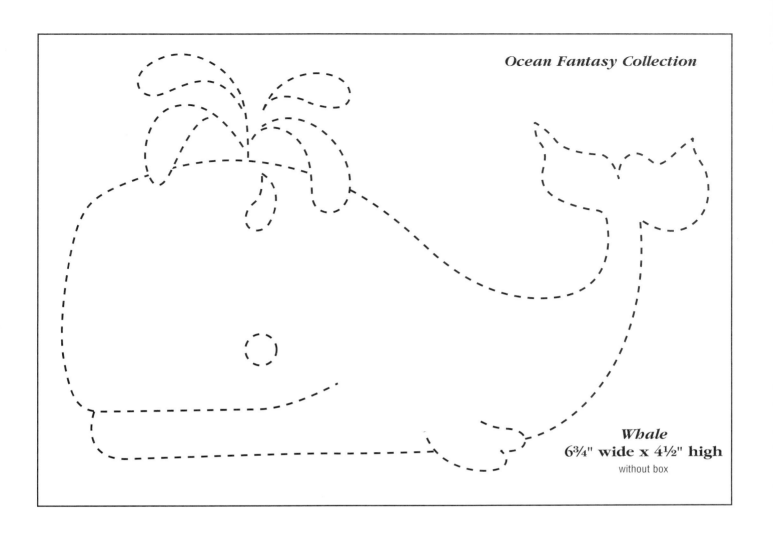

Whale
6¾" wide x 4½" high
without box

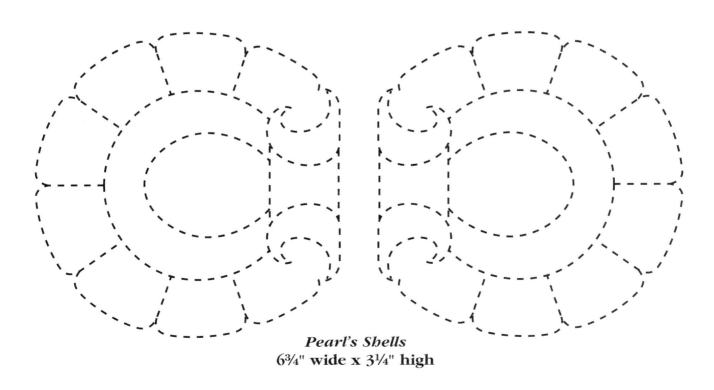

Pearl's Shells
6¾" wide x 3¼" high

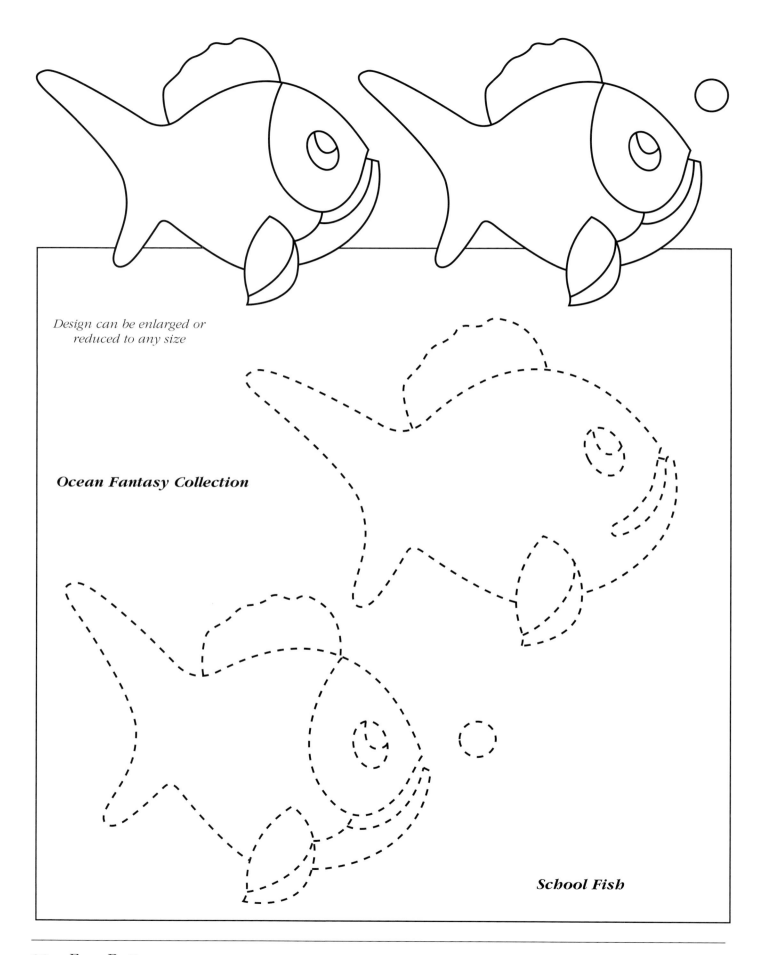

Design can be enlarged or
reduced to any size

Ocean Fantasy Collection

School Fish

Charlie
6½" x 6½"
without box

Ocean Fantasy Collection

Mermaid *(Elongated Clam Shell)*

1½"

2½"

Octopus

Placement Diagram

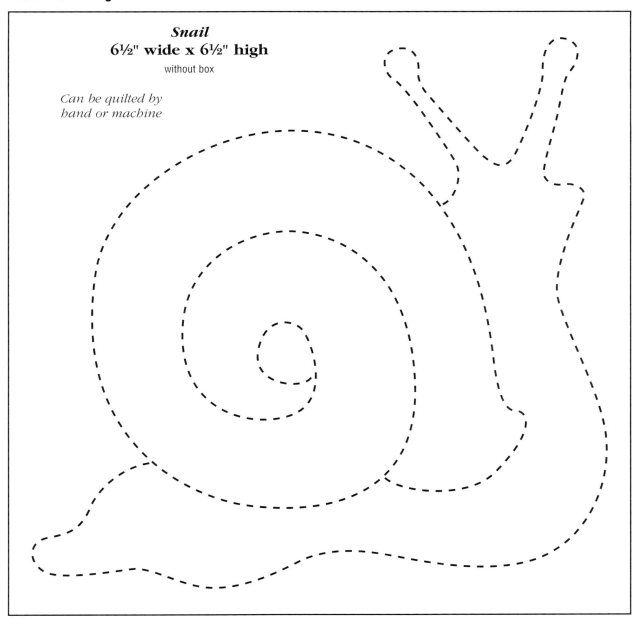

Snail
6½" wide x 6½" high
without box

*Can be quilted by
hand or machine*

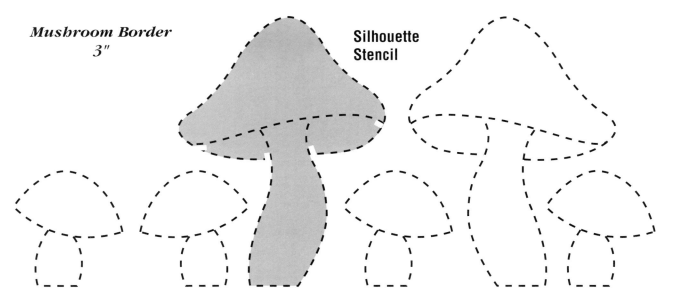

Mushroom Border
3"

Silhouette Stencil

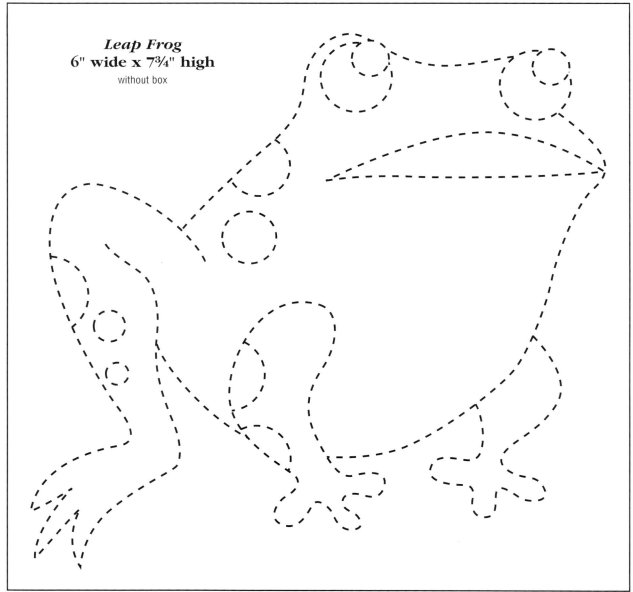

Leap Frog
6" wide x 7¾" high
without box

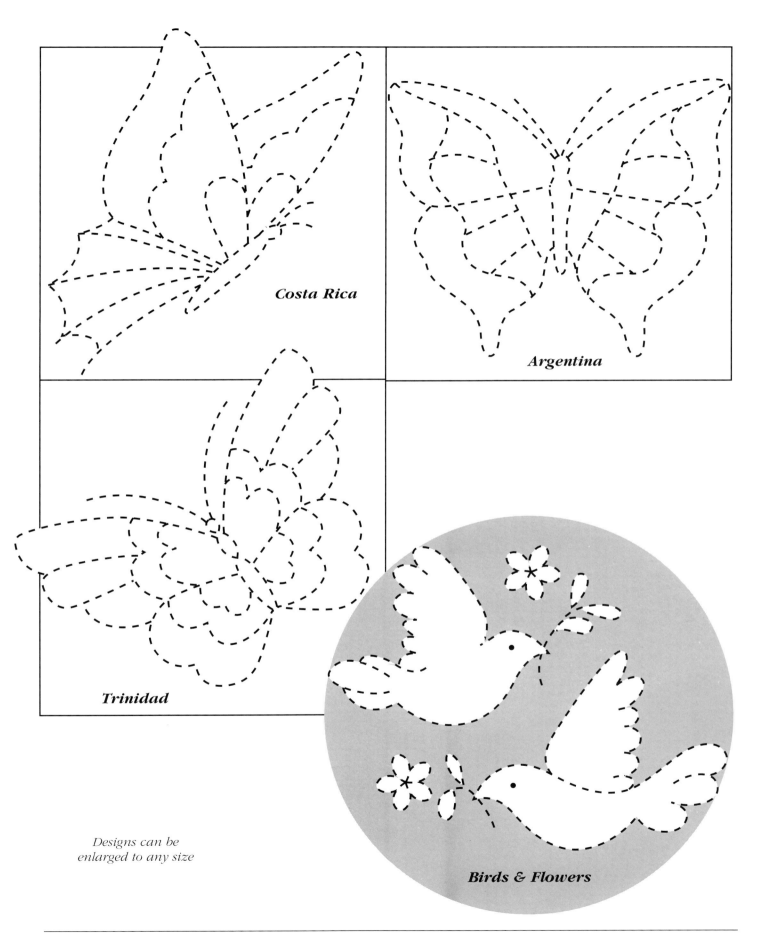

Costa Rica

Argentina

Trinidad

Designs can be enlarged to any size

Birds & Flowers

Helen's Copy & Use Quilting Patterns – Helen Squire

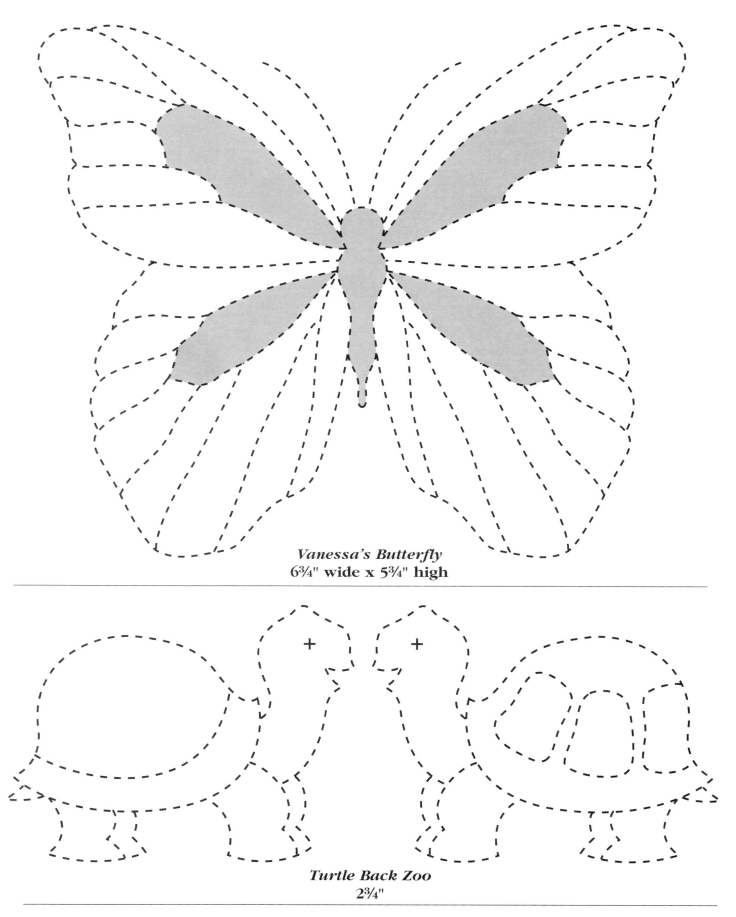

Vanessa's Butterfly
6¾" wide x 5¾" high

Turtle Back Zoo
2¾"

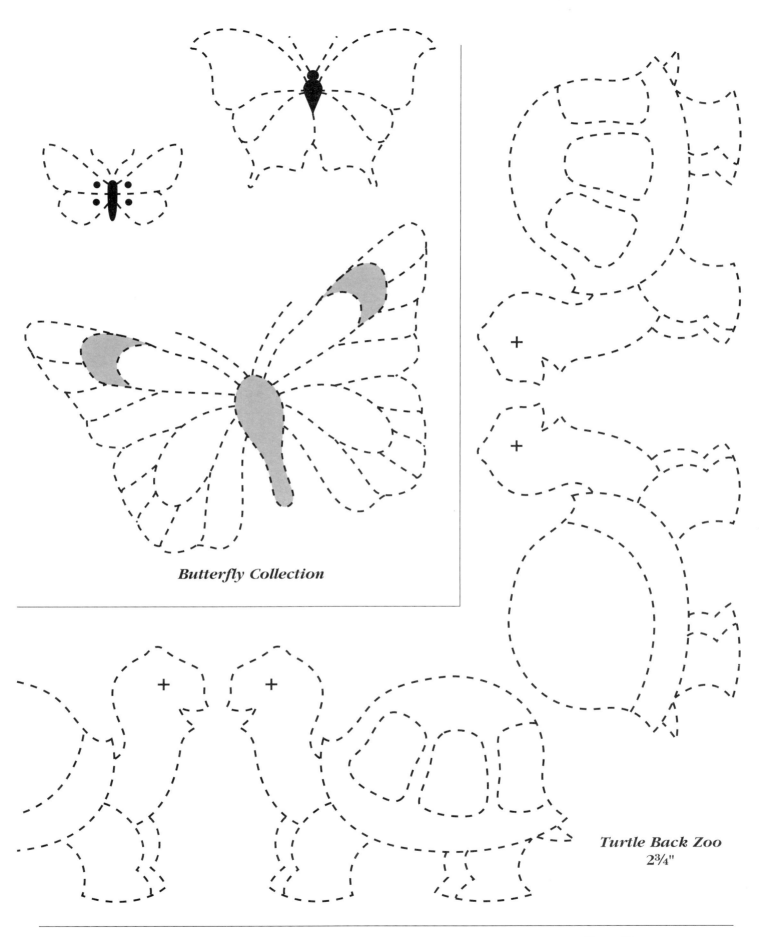

Butterfly Collection

Turtle Back Zoo
2¾"

Chapter Seven

▶ Continuous Lines

☐ Inspired by the silhouette shapes of old cardboard cut-outs, I realized how easy it was to design and mark quilting patterns that could flip & flop, reverse, intertwine & interlock, and adjust to any size quilt.

☐ In 1979, my first group of patterns was printed on heavy manila paper and sold as Quilt-In Design Stencils, shown on next page. Those original nine patterns are still being used by today's quilters!

Placement Diagram

Barbara
8½" wide x 6½" high

dedicated to Barbara Irene Gabrielsen Kelly

Placement Diagram

Jeanne
6½" wide x 5¾" high

dedicated to Jean Anne Gabrielsen Droptiny

Helen's Copy & Use Quilting Patterns – Helen Squire

3" wide

9¼" high

Florence

dedicated to Florence Mae Gabrielsen Andrade

Placement Diagram: Reposition and connect repeats to create an entirely different design.

Carter's Crown
7¼"

Little Angel
7"

Placement Diagram: *Cupid's Wings*

Placement Diagram: *Little Angel*

Cupid's Wings 7"

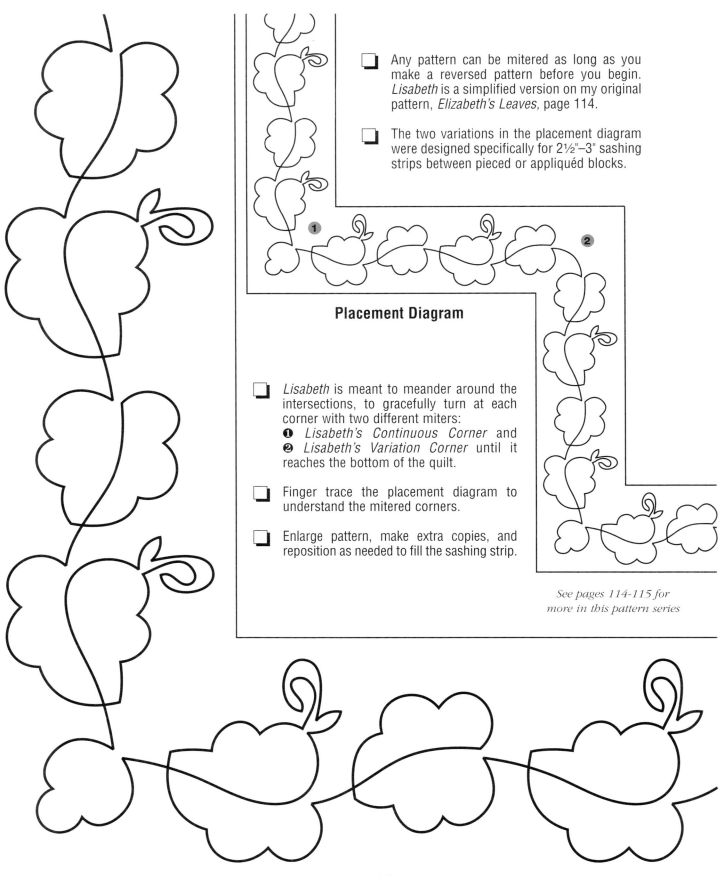

Any pattern can be mitered as long as you make a reversed pattern before you begin. *Lisabeth* is a simplified version on my original pattern, *Elizabeth's Leaves*, page 114.

The two variations in the placement diagram were designed specifically for 2½"–3" sashing strips between pieced or appliquéd blocks.

Placement Diagram

Lisabeth is meant to meander around the intersections, to gracefully turn at each corner with two different miters:
❶ *Lisabeth's Continuous Corner* and
❷ *Lisabeth's Variation Corner* until it reaches the bottom of the quilt.

Finger trace the placement diagram to understand the mitered corners.

Enlarge pattern, make extra copies, and reposition as needed to fill the sashing strip.

See pages 114-115 for more in this pattern series

Lisabeth's Continuous Corner
2¼"

Pattern can be enlarged
or reduced to any size

**Koren's
Border**
4½"

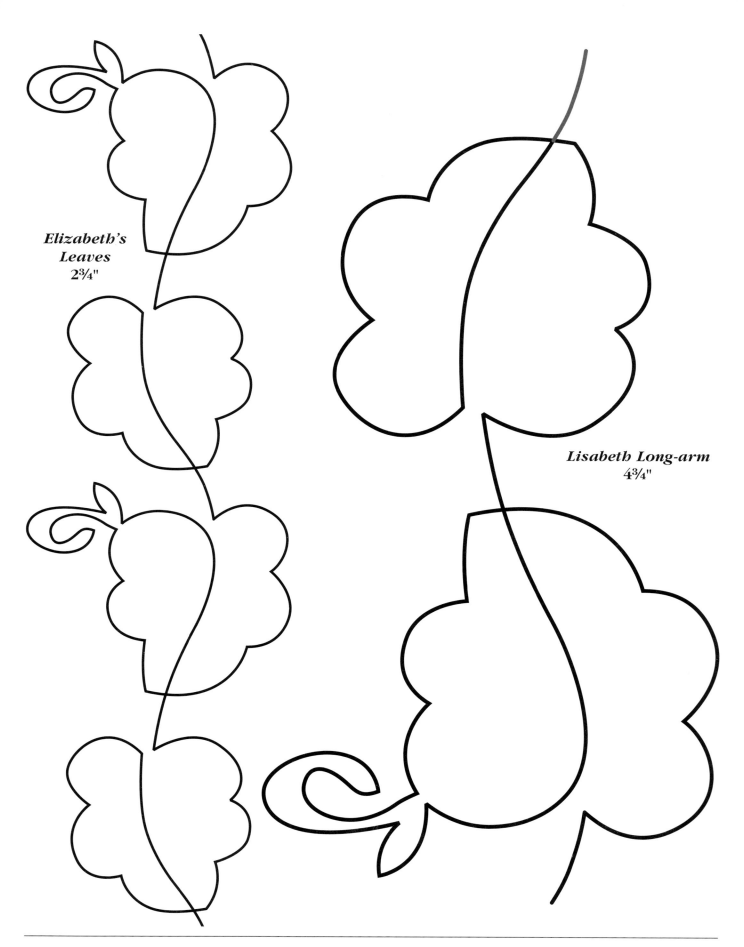

*Elizabeth's
Leaves
2¾"*

*Lisabeth Long-arm
4¾"*

Helen's Copy & Use Quilting Patterns – Helen Squire

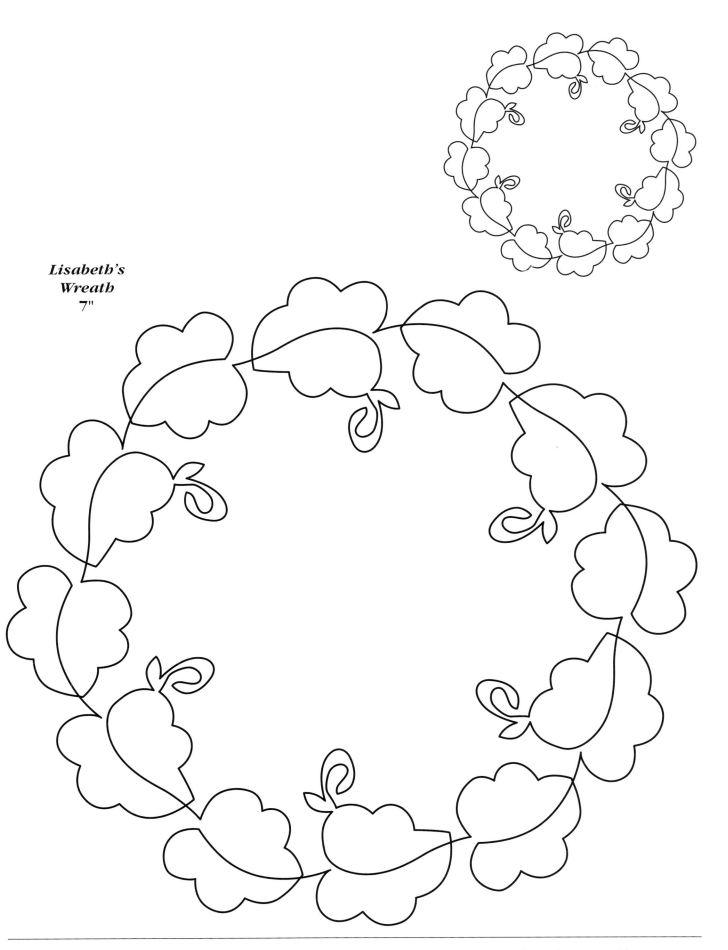

Lisabeth's Wreath 7"

Placement Diagram: Alternate placement of the repeat creates entirely different looks.

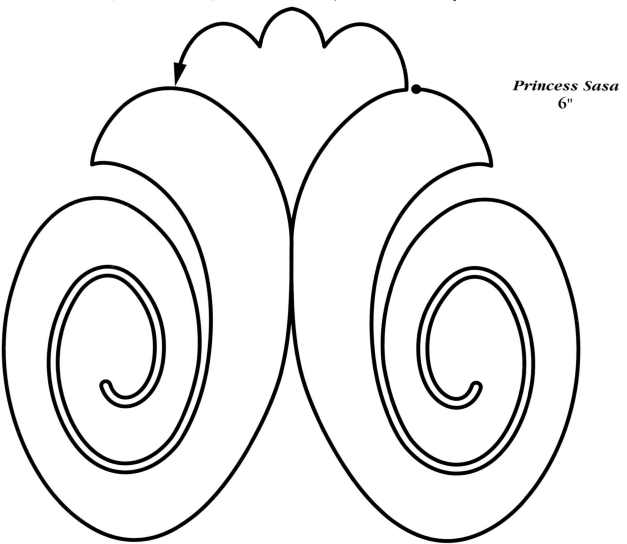

Princess Sasa
6"

Helen's Copy & Use Quilting Patterns – Helen Squire

▲
Placement Diagrams
▼

Helen's Copy & Use Quilting Patterns – Helen Squire

Cloud Nine Traditional

Cloud Nine Appliqué Variation

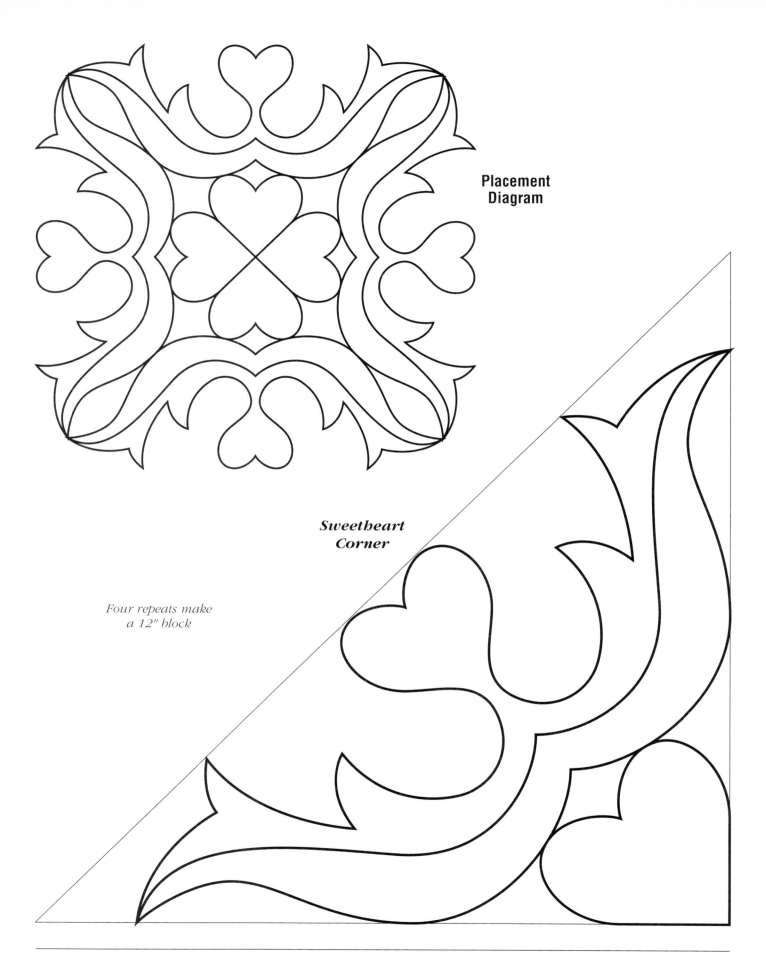

**Placement
Diagram**

*Sweetheart
Corner*

*Four repeats make
a 12" block*

*Baby
Sweetheart
Swag
Long-arm
3"*

Placement Diagram: Machine quilting

Step #1

Step #2

Finished

Placement Diagram

Marilyn
7¼"

Can be enlarged to any size

Helen's Copy & Use Quilting Patterns – Helen Squire

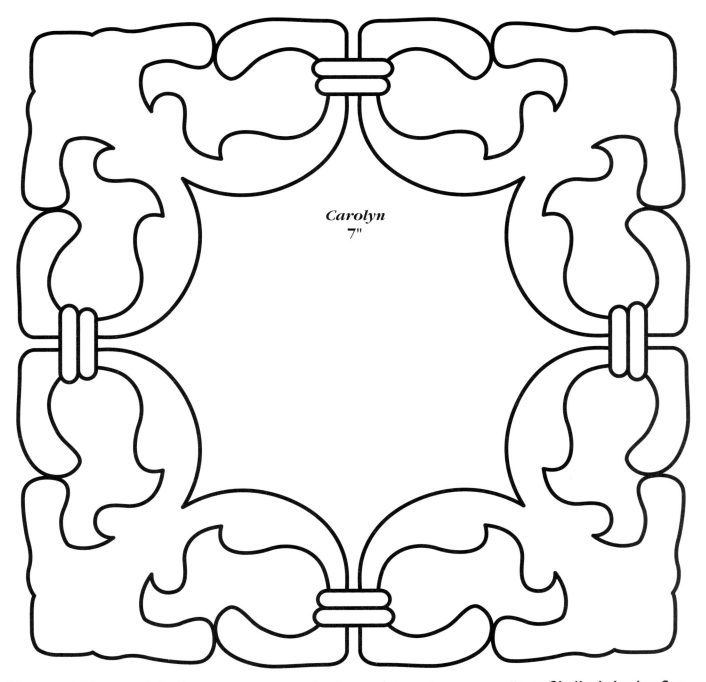

Carolyn
7"

Placement Diagram: Selecting one corner repeat set on-point creates a new pattern, *Shelley's Loving Cup*.

Chapter Eight

Elegant Sets

☐ The beauty of this elegant pattern lies in its ability to transform into companion variations.

☐ I have always been able to re-position or miter any design at least four different ways, but with *Theresa's Scroll & Leaf,* it was easy to find nine different design potentials! The difficulty was in deciding which ones to showcase.

Elegant Block
7¼"

Helen's Copy & Use Quilting Patterns – Helen Squire

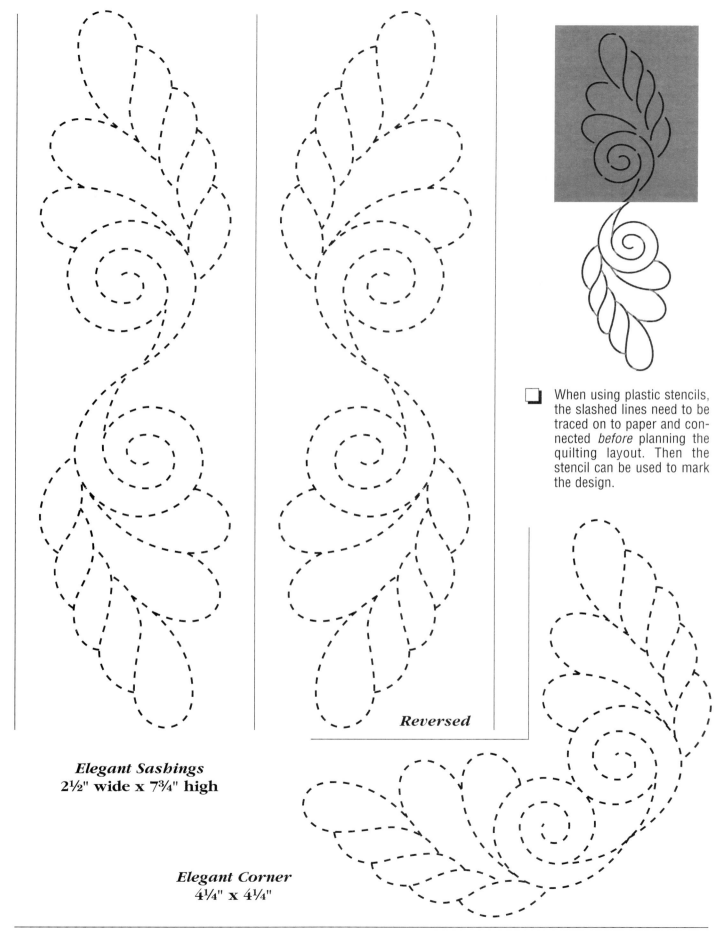

When using plastic stencils, the slashed lines need to be traced on to paper and connected *before* planning the quilting layout. Then the stencil can be used to mark the design.

Reversed

Elegant Sashings
2½" wide x 7¾" high

Elegant Corner
4¼" x 4¼"

Companion pattern
Elegant Swirl,
page 25.

Lily Pad Swag
9 wide x 3¼" high

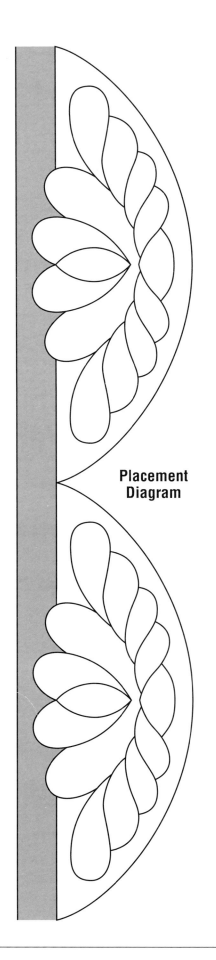

**Placement
Diagram**

Backgrounds can be machine stippled to flatten that area, thereby raising the *Elegant Corner* motif.

Elegant Rope
1¼"

Orig 1¼"   1½ = 120% 1¾ = 140%

3¼ = 260%

Elegant Heart Center
8½" wide x 3" high

Elegant Center
6" wide x 2" high

Elegant Heart Block with Grid 7¼"

Helen's Copy & Use Quilting Patterns – Helen Squire

Francine

Placement Diagram

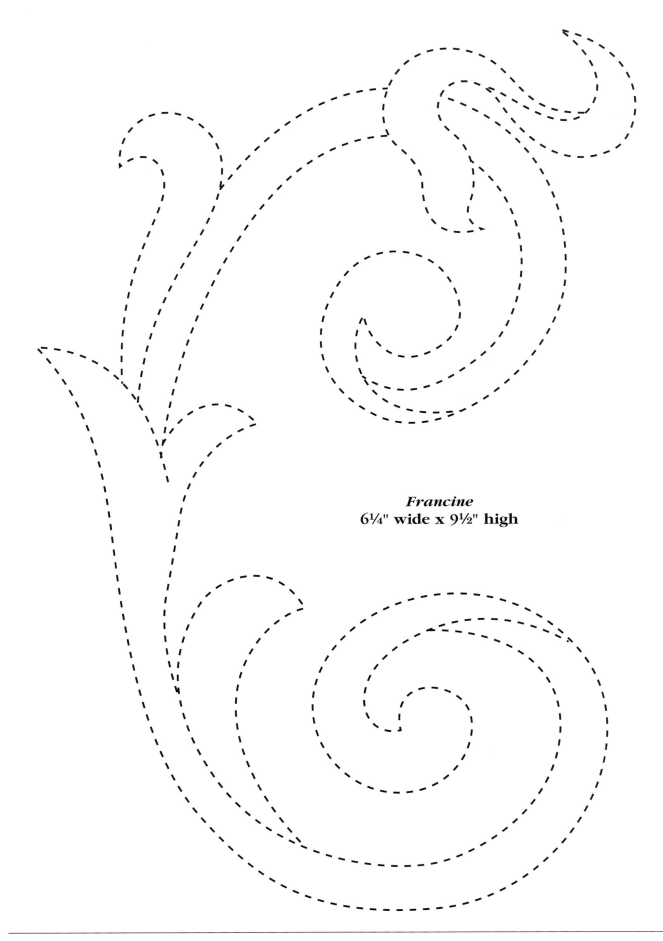

Francine
6¼" wide x 9½" high

Elisa's Posie Basket
7¼"

Placement Diagram

To emphasize the most predominant part of the quilting design: ❶ Enlarge the pattern to fit the area to be quilted; ❷ make sure the background does not overwhelm the design; ❸ add filler stitches. Stippling would effectively reduce and flatten the openness behind the basket.

Use the design's motifs to break up the shaded area. The leaves have been lifted and laid on top of the *Phyllis' Philodendron* corner pieces, page 133, thereby dividing the background into smaller segments.

The main design, *Elisa's Posie Basket*, now dominates the quilting area. The basket has been anchored, so it does not appear to float in space.

Narrow Band

Combination

Wide Band

Phyllis' Philodendron
7"

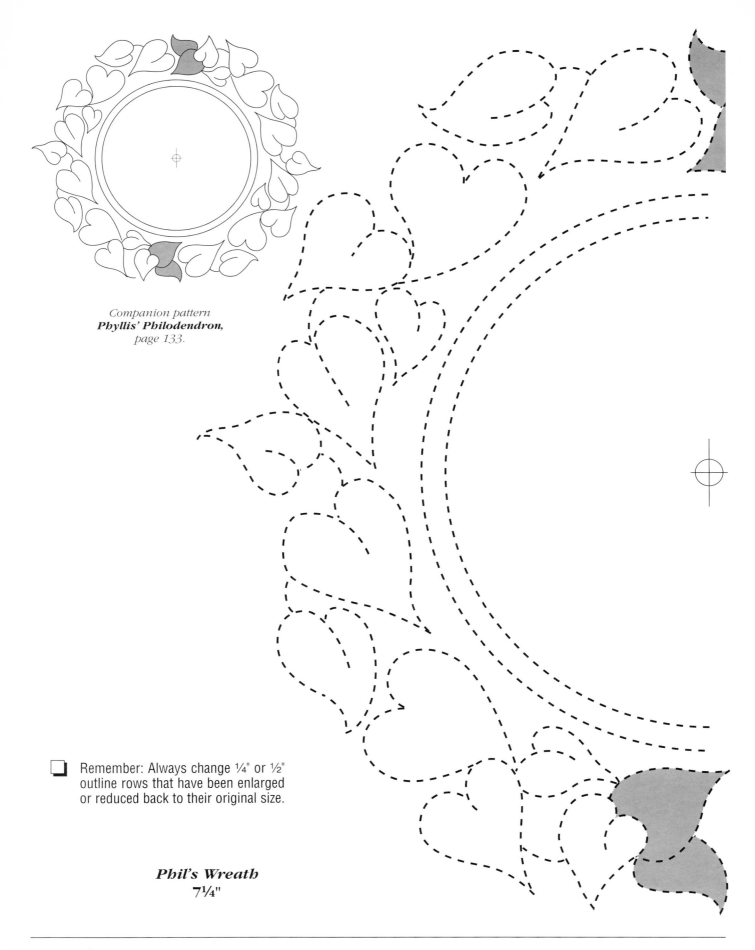

Companion pattern
Phyllis' Philodendron,
page 133.

Remember: Always change ¼" or ½"
outline rows that have been enlarged
or reduced back to their original size.

Phil's Wreath
7¼"

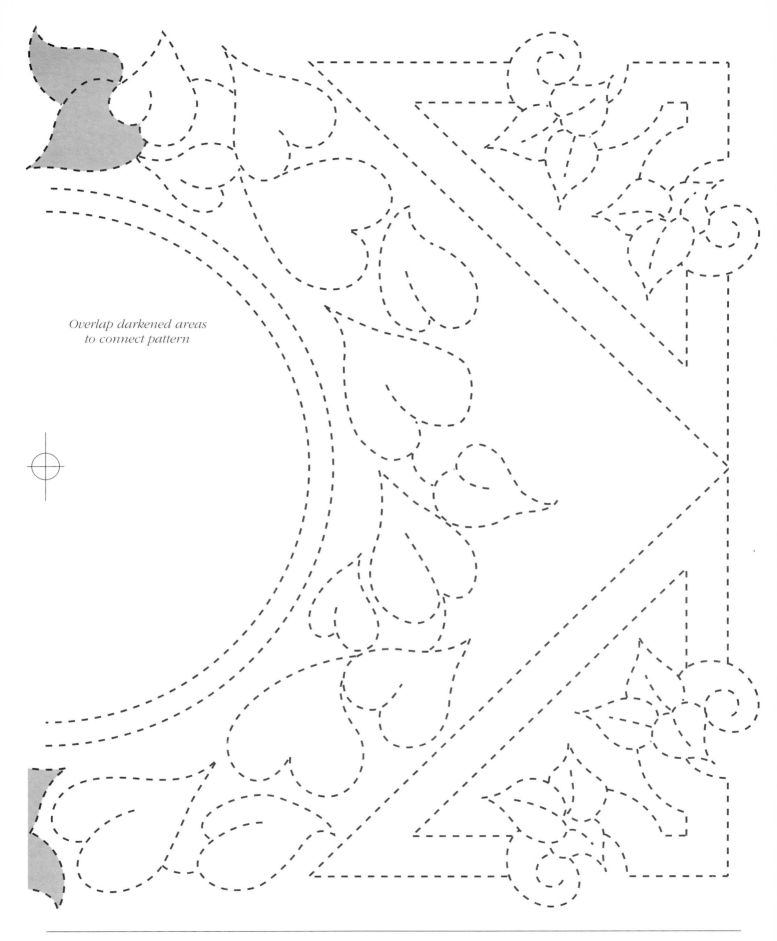

Overlap darkened areas
to connect pattern

Placement Diagram

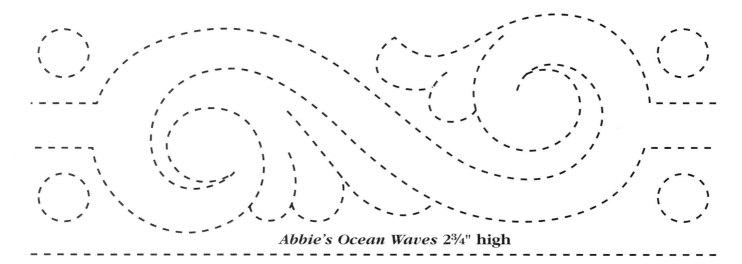

Abbie's Ocean Waves 2¾" **high**

Placement Diagram

connect here

Manie's Maui
12½" **wide**

Surfs Up
Continuous Line

connect here

Manie's Maui
reversed

Chapter Nine

Grids VI

On the following pages are standard background grids:
½" crosshatch
¾" crosshatch
1" crosshatch

Pumpkin Seed
1¾" Circle

■ Grids have to be very accurate. Do *not* make photocopies, which can distort the grid lines.

■ Redraft additional sheets or sizes (use indelible ink to prevent pencil smudges) and tape extra pages together for larger area.

Pumpkin Seed
1¾" Circle

Gladys' Rose
9½" wide x 5" high

Other AQS Books

This is only a small selection of the books available from the American Quilter's Society. AQS books are known worldwide for timely topics, clear writing, beautiful color photos, and accurate illustrations and patterns. The following books are available from your local bookseller, quilt shop, or the public library.

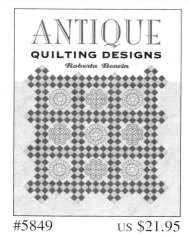

#5849   US $21.95

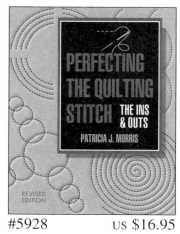

#5928   US $16.95

#4628 17"x 11"   US $16.95

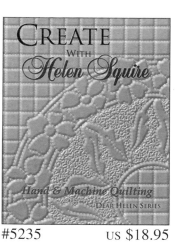

#5235   US $18.95

#5817 14"x 11"   US $16.95

#4818 17"x 11"   US $15.95

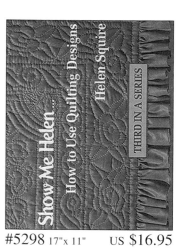

#5298 17"x 11"   US $16.95

#3470 9¼"x 12¼"   US $24.95

#2099 17"x 11"   US $14.95

Look for these books nationally or call **1-800-626-5420**